# KKEY DATA ON ADADOLESCENCESCENCE 2009

John Coleman
Fiona Brooks

With:
Ellen Klemera
Jane Schofield
Daksha Trivedi

Trust for the

Study of

Adolescence

ayph | Association for
Young People's Health

1317139q

Published by AYPH Ltd and TSA Ltd.
© AYPH Ltd and TSA Ltd.  2009

British Library Cataloguing-in-Publication Data.
A catalogue record for this book is available from the British Library.

ISBN: 978 187 1504 965

Design: Helen Beauvais
Printed by: Creative Media Colour Ltd. Tel: 01273 555590

# PREFACE

## The Association for Young People's Health (AYPH)

AYPH is a major new charity and membership organisation founded in 2008. It aims to create a focus for all professionals and organisations working in the field of young people's health. It promotes multi-disciplinary training; advocates for improvements in young people's health services; disseminates information; and supports research.

AYPH, PO Box 5229, Brighton, BN50 9YR
Email: info@youngpeopleshealth.org.uk
Website: www.youngpeopleshealth.org.uk

## Trust for the Study of Adolescence (TSA)

TSA is a national charity founded in 1989. It aims to improve the lives of young people and families by providing professionals with the knowledge, skills and resources they need to provide better services. Its work includes: projects that develop professional practice; research and evaluation; producing practical resources; training professionals; influencing policy makers.

TSA, 23 New Road, Brighton, BN1 1WZ
Tel: +44(0)1273 693311 Fax: +44(0)1273 679907
Email: info@tsa.uk.com
Website: www.tsa.uk.com

## The Authors

Dr John Coleman has been the author of all previous editions of Key Data on Adolescence. He is a Senior Research Fellow in the Department of Education in the University of Oxford and the Chair of the Association for Young People's Health (AYPH). He has written widely about adolescence, founded the Trust for the Study of Adolescence (TSA) and was its Director, 1989-2005. John was awarded an OBE in 2001 for services to youth.

Professor Fiona Brooks is a medical sociologist and programme lead for the CRIPACC adolescent and child health research group (University of Hertfordshire). She has a long-standing interest in the impact of policy developments on health care, including the implications of innovative service developments and user empowerment.

# ACKNOWLEDGEMENTS

The preparation of this publication would not have been possible without the assistance of many people. We would particularly like to thank Angela and John Balding, of the University of Exeter, Keith Hawton and his colleagues of the University of Oxford, Ann McPherson and Aidan Macfarlane, creators of the website "Teenage Health Freak", and Anthony Morgan, author of reports on the Health Behaviour of School Aged Children (HBSC) study. In addition, Debi Roker and the staff team at the Trust for the Study of Adolescence have given invaluable assistance, as have the Committee members of the Association for Young People's Health. The authors would like to express their gratitude to Paul Treadgold, who has developed the Key Messages and contributed in many other ways to the final version. Finally, a special thank you goes to Jane Schofield. In her role as Production Manager she has overseen every stage of the process. This publication would not have been possible without her commitment and perseverance.

**John Coleman**
**Fiona Brooks**

# INTRODUCTION

## Introduction to the 7th Edition of Key Data on Adolescence

It is now 12 years since the first edition of this volume appeared, and we are proud of our record in making publicly available important data on young people in Britain over the past decade. When we started off on this venture we did not imagine that it would continue in this way, but the demand for such a volume has not grown any the less since the first edition appeared.

From the beginning, we have seen this book as a resource for students, journalists, practitioners, researchers and policy makers looking for answers to important questions about the lives of young people. While much has changed for adolescents and their families over twelve years, the need for good quality information remains an absolute priority for all who engage with young people at school, in the community or at home.

Since 1997, this volume has been published by the Trust for the Study of Adolescence (TSA). The current volume represents a new departure in that it is a joint venture with a new organisation, the Association for Young People's Health (AYPH). We are delighted that such a collaboration has been possible, and the shared commitment and breadth of interest of the two organisations has given this volume a new impetus and, of course, an increased focus on health issues. We have also benefited hugely from the fact that the research has been carried out by Fiona Brooks' team at the University of Hertfordshire. We have already made proper acknowledgement of the role played by the researchers in the title page, but we do wish to underline the extent to which this volume has been a shared project between TSA, AYPH and the University of Hertfordshire. We believe the collaboration has greatly added to the strength of this publication.

The overall message from this edition of Key Data on Adolescence is, inevitably, a mixed one. There are some "good news" messages, and we believe it is important to underline these. For example, the decline in the rate of suicide among young men, and the reduction in the rates of offending among this group, are facts that should be widely acknowledged. Conception rates among young women have also fallen, as have the numbers of young people who are smoking cigarettes. However alcohol use has increased substantially among the young and, in terms of poverty, Britain still compares very poorly with other European countries when it comes to the numbers living in disadvantaged families. One theme running through this volume has to do with gender comparisons, and we have been struck by the greater degree of health risk to which girls are exposed. They take less exercise than boys, they smoke more than boys, and their use of alcohol has risen markedly over the last decade.

Our final point has to do with the inadequacy of the data available on many aspects of adolescent health. Frequently statistics are recorded in ways that make it impossible to draw sensible conclusions as, for example, collecting data on those between 0 and 19, or on those from 14 to 59. We wish to express our concern that more effort should be made to collect good data on the health and health behaviour of young people. Unless attention is paid to this, it will be difficult to introduce real improvements in services for this age group.

**John Coleman**
**Fiona Brooks**

# CONTENTS

**Preface**

**Acknowledgements**

**Introduction**

## 1:  Population, Families and Households

### Population

### Families and households

### Looked after children, young people and asylum seekers

## 2:  Education, Training and Employment

## 3:  Primary Health Care and Health Behaviours

## 4:  Secondary Care, Long-term Conditions and Disability

## 5:  Sexual Health

## 6:  Mental Health

## 7: Crime

# CHAPTER 1

# Population, Families and Households

KEY MESSAGES

## Increase in number of adolescents

The number of adolescents aged 10-19 living in the UK has increased by more than 11% since 1995 to around 7.8 million today (Chart 1.1)

## High proportion in lone parent families

One in four of all children and young people in the UK now live in households headed by a lone parent (Chart 1.5)

## 1.8 million in workless households

Over 16% of children aged 0-17 live in workless households. This is much higher than in other European countries and almost twice the EU average (Chart 1.11)

## Young adults living at home for longer

Over 50% of young men and just under 40% of young women in Britain aged 20-24 are still living in their family home (Chart 1.13)

## Population, Families and Households

As a background to a consideration of young people's place in society, it is helpful to commence with a look at the population figures. As can be seen in **Chart 1.1** there are approximately 7.8 million 10-19 year-olds currently living in the UK. Children under 10 number 7.0 million, so there are rather more adolescents than children in the population at present. It should be noted that there has been a gradual increase in the number of teenagers in the last decade or so, together with a corresponding decrease in the number of children. Thus in 1995 there were 7.6 million children and only 7.0 million adolescents, a somewhat different picture to the one we see today. The increase in the number of teenagers clearly has important implications for policy, as well as for the provision of public services such as education, health and youth work.

If comparisons are made with older age bands it can be seen that the numbers are significantly higher among 30-39 year-olds, where there is a total of 8.3 million, and among 40-49 year-olds, where there is a total of 9.0 million. It should also be noted that children and adolescents make up roughly a quarter of the population of the United Kingdom, a proportion that is similar to other European countries. However, in countries in the developing world the child and adolescent population is more likely to be half of the total, or even more in some parts of Africa and South America.

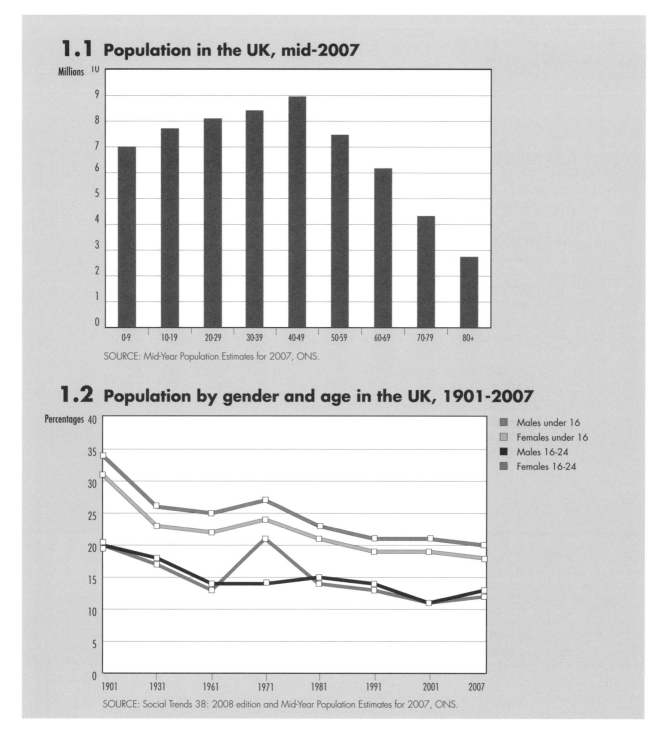

### 1.1 Population in the UK, mid-2007

Millions

SOURCE: Mid-Year Population Estimates for 2007, ONS.

### 1.2 Population by gender and age in the UK, 1901-2007

Percentages

■ Males under 16
□ Females under 16
■ Males 16-24
■ Females 16-24

SOURCE: Social Trends 38: 2008 edition and Mid-Year Population Estimates for 2007, ONS.

## 1.3 Population in England by ethnic group, 2006

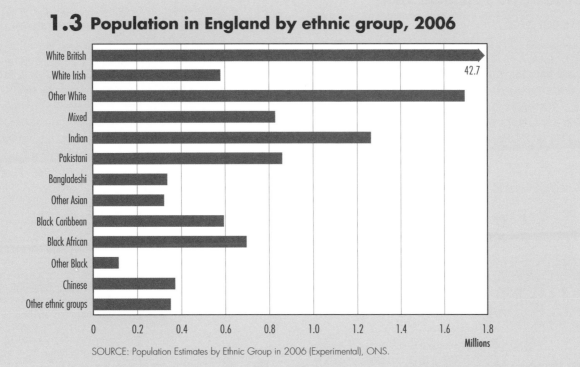

SOURCE: Population Estimates by Ethnic Group in 2006 (Experimental), ONS.

## 1.4 Population by ethnic group and age in England, 2006

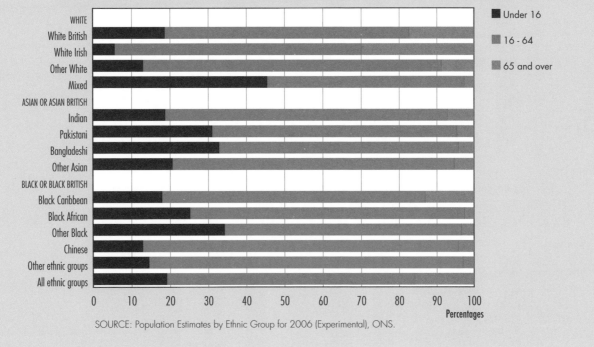

SOURCE: Population Estimates by Ethnic Group for 2006 (Experimental), ONS.

As far as historical change is concerned, it can be seen from **Chart 1.2** that the proportion of both under-16s and 16-24 year-olds in the population has fallen steadily over a century. By contrast, the proportion of those in all age groups over the age of 25 has increased during this period, with the sharpest increases coming in the older age groups. It will be clear that these demographic trends have major implications for public policy. As the demand for services for the older age groups continues to grow, so it will become more difficult to find resources to meet the needs of children and adolescents.

Turning to race and ethnicity, it can be seen from **Chart 1.3** that in 2006, in England, ethnic minority groups accounted for approximately 5.5 million out of a total population of 50 million. As is apparent from data in **Chart 1.4** there are wide variations in the age distribution of different populations. This is most marked in the Mixed group, those from Pakistani and Bangladeshi origins, and those classified as Other Black, in which groups can be found the highest proportions of those who are under 16.

## Families and Households

During the last 40 years, there have been a number of trends in relation to families and households which are important to recognise and which have had substantial impacts on the adolescent population. These trends include a decrease in the stability of marriage and an increase in partnerships and parenthood outside marriage. The change in family composition between 1971 and 2006 is shown clearly in **Chart 1.5**. Here it can be seen that the number of families with dependent children headed by a lone parent has increased from 8% of all families in 1971 to 25% of all families in 2006. In fact, a slightly higher proportion, at 27%, was seen in 2002 but the proportion stabilised at 25% over the four years which followed. The overall increase over the 35 year period represents a major social change, and one that has relevance not only for childcare, for welfare provision and for the economy, but also for the very nature of parenthood.

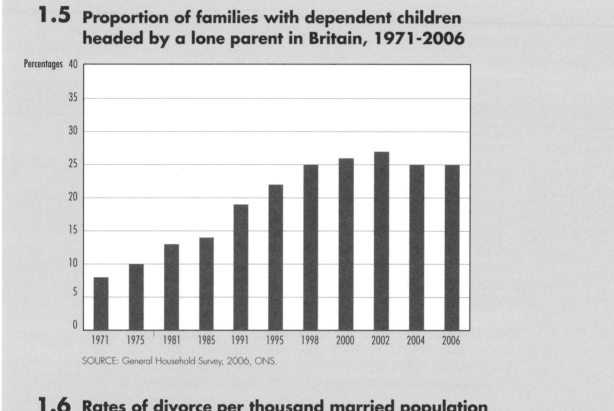

**1.5** **Proportion of families with dependent children headed by a lone parent in Britain, 1971-2006**

SOURCE: General Household Survey, 2006, ONS.

**1.6** **Rates of divorce per thousand married population in England and Wales, 1985-2005**

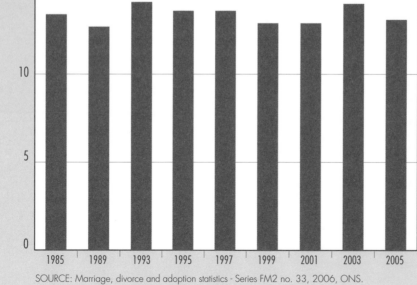

SOURCE: Marriage, divorce and adoption statistics - Series FM2 no. 33, 2006, ONS.

## 1.7 Families with dependent children headed by lone mothers, by circumstance, 1971-2006

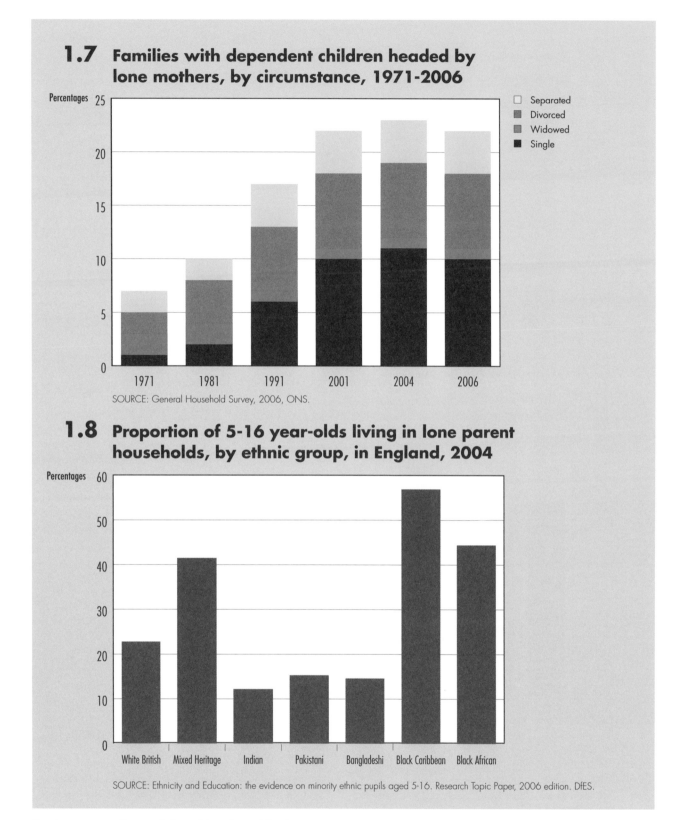

Percentages

Legend:
☐ Separated
▨ Divorced
▨ Widowed
■ Single

1971   1981   1991   2001   2004   2006

SOURCE: General Household Survey, 2006, ONS.

## 1.8 Proportion of 5-16 year-olds living in lone parent households, by ethnic group, in England, 2004

Percentages

White British   Mixed Heritage   Indian   Pakistani   Bangladeshi   Black Caribbean   Black African

SOURCE: Ethnicity and Education: the evidence on minority ethnic pupils aged 5-16. Research Topic Paper, 2006 edition. DfES.

Turning now to divorce, it is striking that while the number of lone parent families has been increasing, the rates of divorce have remained relatively stable over the last 20 years or so. As can be seen from **Chart 1.6**, rates of divorce in England and Wales have fluctuated somewhat but have stayed between 12.7 and 14.1 per thousand married population in the two decades between 1985 and 2005.

The increase in lone parent families is explained if we take into account that not all such families come into being because of divorce. Figures in **Chart 1.7** illustrate this fact. Here it can be seen that the group that has increased most is the single group, thus contributing to the rise in families headed by a lone parent. It is also important to consider ethnicity when looking at the distribution of family types in Britain. Figures in **Chart 1.8** show that lone parent families are not equally distributed across cultures. Numbers of lone parent families are significantly higher among Black Caribbean, Black African and mixed ethnic groups.

## 1.9 Gross weekly income of families with dependent children, by family type in Britain, 2006

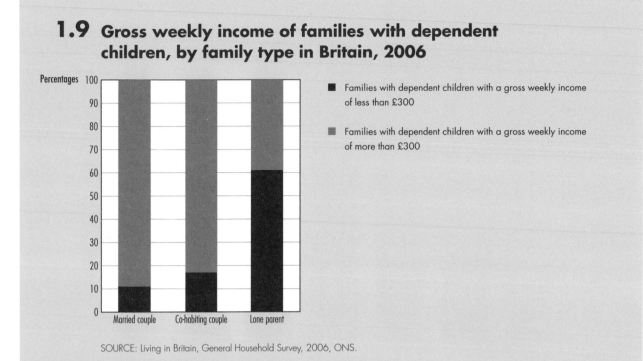

Percentages

- ■ Families with dependent children with a gross weekly income of less than £300
- ■ Families with dependent children with a gross weekly income of more than £300

Married couple    Co-habiting couple    Lone parent

SOURCE: Living in Britain, General Household Survey, 2006, ONS.

## 1.10 Children in workless households in the UK, 1995-2007

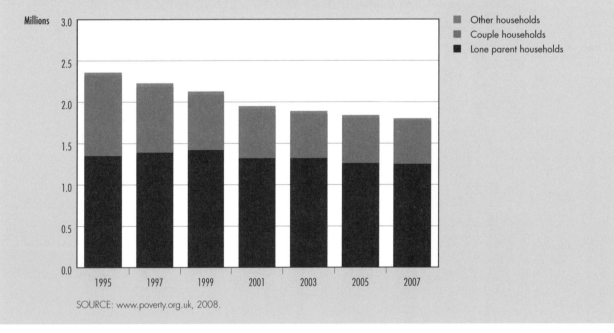

Millions

- ■ Other households
- ■ Couple households
- ■ Lone parent households

SOURCE: www.poverty.org.uk, 2008.

Since 1997, the Labour Government has made much of its commitment to cutting child poverty, and there is no doubt that the fiscal and social programmes designed with this end in mind have had major repercussions for less well-off families in Britain. A dramatic illustration of the link between poverty and family life may be found if average household incomes are compared. In **Chart 1.9** we have drawn a comparison between families with incomes over and under £300 per week. As can be seen, couple families are nearly three times more likely to have weekly incomes over £300 than are lone parent families. The impact of such financial differentials on children and young people cannot be under-estimated.

The scale of the problem is further illustrated in **Chart 1.10** showing the number of children and young people in the UK where there is no parent at work. The numbers of such families fell between 1995 and 2007, with about 1.8 million children in workless households in 2007. What is most striking is the differences between those living in couple families and those living in families headed by a lone parent. In spite of much Government intervention encouraging parents back into work, there still remains a very large gap between parents in different family structures. Lastly on this subject, it is shocking to look at comparisons between the UK and other European countries.

Figures in **Chart 1.11** show how far we lag behind our European counterparts, with over 16% of all children living in workless households in Great Britain in 2007. This is a statistic that rarely gets much attention yet clearly deserves to be the focus of much public concern.

Another very important social change that has occurred since the 1970s is the number of children being born outside marriage. Commentators differ on the specific reasons for this, and it is not clear what reflection this has on current attitudes to marriage.

Undoubtedly, many children born outside marriage will be born to parents living in stable relationships which may, in time, turn into marriages. The high number of children born outside marriage may not necessarily indicate that marriage is out of fashion. Rather, many couples may now wait before getting married and then find that becoming a parent is the spur that makes them feel ready to marry. Figures in **Chart 1.12** illustrate the growing numbers of children who are born outside marriage, the greatest proportion being born to the youngest parents.

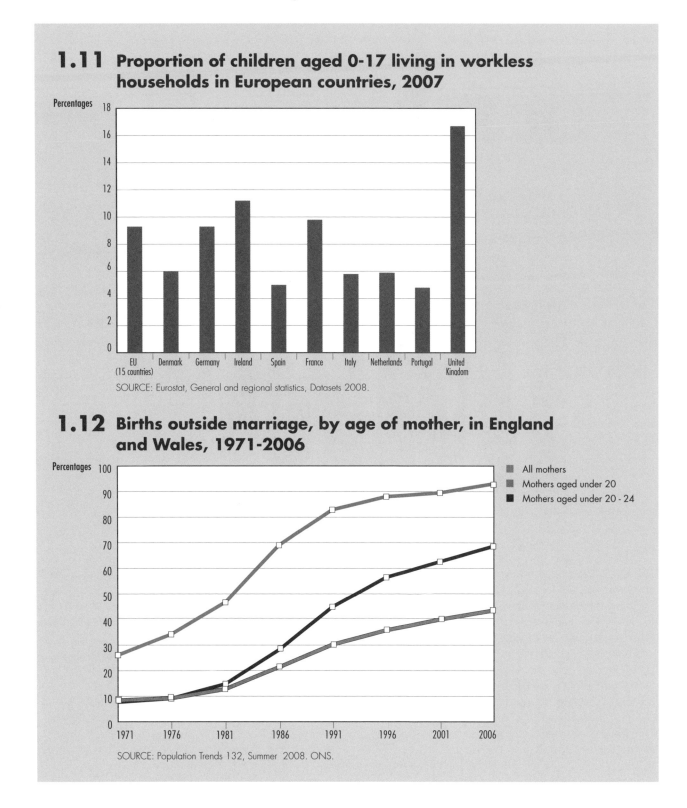

**1.11** **Proportion of children aged 0-17 living in workless households in European countries, 2007**

SOURCE: Eurostat, General and regional statistics, Datasets 2008.

**1.12** **Births outside marriage, by age of mother, in England and Wales, 1971-2006**

All mothers
Mothers aged under 20
Mothers aged under 20 - 24

SOURCE: Population Trends 132, Summer 2008. ONS.

The last question to be considered in this section is that of leaving home. There has been much discussion of the disappearance of the "empty nest", with many young people remaining at home for longer periods, or even returning home after a spell in higher education. The phrase "the crowded nest" has been coined to reflect this changing situation. We will consider some of the possible reasons for this when, in Chapter 2, we discuss the changing nature of the labour market and the lengthening periods of further and higher education experienced by young people today. The most recent figures on this phenomenon appeared in Social Trends 36 (2006) and are illustrated in **Chart 1.13**. These figures show a gradual increase in those staying at home for both men and women under the

age of 30 between 1991 and 2005. Women aged between 25 and 29 are the group showing least change in this respect.

Comparisons of numbers staying in the family home across European countries have become available through the Eurostat publication, and these show that in Britain there are a high number of young adults remaining at home, although not as high as in some other European countries such as Italy and Spain. In Britain, as in other countries, there are more young men than young women who live with their parents, 65% of those between the ages of 18 and 24. This figure diminishes to 23% in the older age group. Comparisons can be seen in **Charts 1.14** and **1.15**.

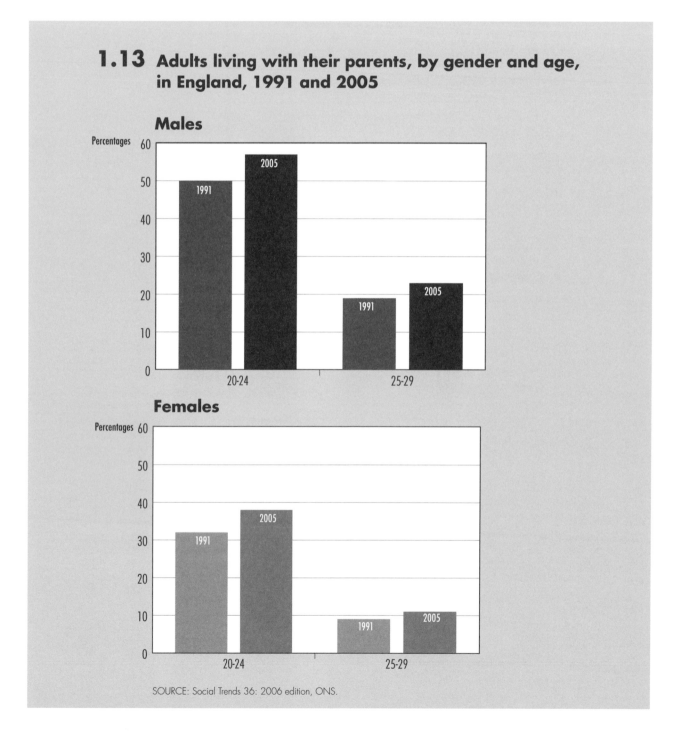

## 1.13 Adults living with their parents, by gender and age, in England, 1991 and 2005

**Males**

Percentages

**Females**

Percentages

SOURCE: Social Trends 36: 2006 edition, ONS.

## 1.14 Percentage of young men living with their parents in different European countries, 2005

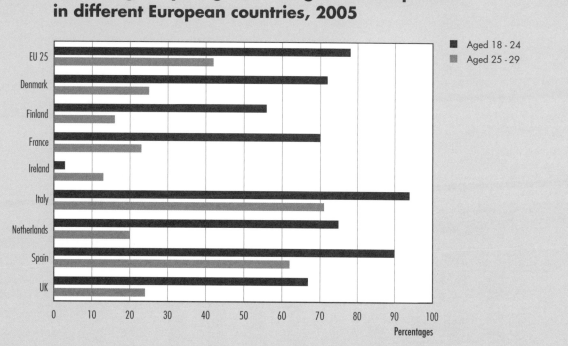

SOURCE: The life of women and men in Europe. A statistical portrait. Eurostat statistical book, 2008 edition.

## 1.15 Percentage of young women living with their parents in different European countries, 2005

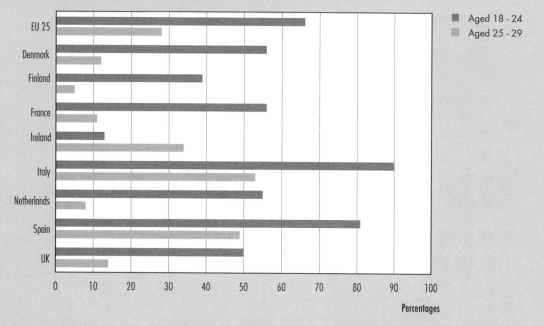

SOURCE: The life of women and men in Europe. A statistical portrait. Eurostat statistical book, 2008 edition.

## Looked after Children and Young People, and Asylum Seekers

We will first consider looked after children and young people. Although the numbers may be relatively small, children and young people looked after by the local authority are a significant minority, perhaps most importantly because of their vulnerability. This group, as we shall see, does poorly on almost all outcome

measures, including school performance, mental health, involvement with the criminal justice system and employment. Over the last decade, Government has recognised the extent of the problem and made many attempts to address some of the challenges involved. Sadly the problems are not easy to overcome, and research on outcomes today does not show a particularly encouraging picture.

In terms of numbers, the figures available are based on a snapshot over a census week, and we return to the interpretation of these data below. Although there was a steady reduction among the looked after

### 1.16 Children in care/looked after in England, 1991-2007

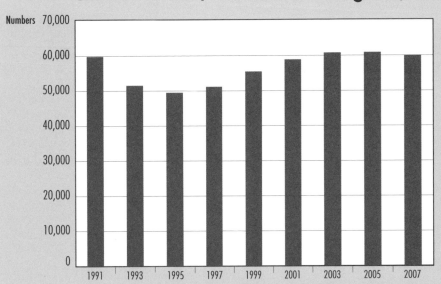

SOURCE: Children looked after by local authorities, year ending 31 March 2005 and Children looked after in England, year ending 31 March 2007, DfES.

### 1.17 Children in care/looked after in England, by gender, 1990-2006

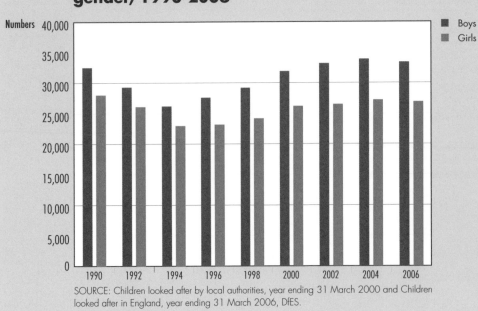

SOURCE: Children looked after by local authorities, year ending 31 March 2000 and Children looked after in England, year ending 31 March 2006, DfES.

population during the early 1990s, it can be seen from figures in **Chart 1.16** that this trend has been reversed since 1997. In the decade since then, numbers have risen by approximately 10,000. It is important to recognise that the figures shown in **Chart 1.16** are a snapshot only and do not fully reflect the whole picture. Factors that need to be taken into account are the numbers looked after during a whole year, as well as the average length of stay in local authority care. It seems probable that the reason for the increase in rates is because of longer stays in care, rather than because of any actual increase in absolute numbers.

As far as gender is concerned, figures in **Chart 1.17** show that boys have always outnumbered girls in this group, and there appears to be a trend towards greater gender inequality from about 1998 onwards. In 2006 in England, there was a total of 33,400 males in care, as opposed to 'only' 26,900 females. It is often assumed that large proportions of children and young people in care are from minority backgrounds. Figures illustrated in **Chart 1.18** show that the great majority of such individuals are from White backgrounds, but there are clearly significant numbers from other backgrounds. The distribution can be seen to spread across many cultural groups.

## 1.18 Children looked after in England by ethnic origin, 2003-2007

Numbers

| | 2003 | 2004 | 2005 | 2006 | 2007 |
|---|---|---|---|---|---|
| **White** | | | | | |
| White British | 47,300 | 46,300 | 45,900 | 45,000 | 44,700 |
| White Irish | 580 | 520 | 500 | 440 | 400 |
| Any other White background | 1,800 | 1,900 | 1,800 | 1,600 | 1,500 |
| **Mixed** | | | | | |
| White and Black Caribbean | 2,000 | 2,000 | 2,000 | 1,900 | 1,900 |
| White and Black African | 400 | 410 | 440 | 430 | 440 |
| White and Asian | 750 | 720 | 720 | 750 | 770 |
| Any other mixed background | 2,000 | 2,000 | 2,000 | 2,000 | 2,000 |
| **Asian or Asian British** | | | | | |
| Indian | 300 | 300 | 280 | 300 | 290 |
| Pakistani | 510 | 520 | 580 | 610 | 660 |
| Bangladeshi | 200 | 230 | 270 | 280 | 280 |
| Any other Asian background | 320 | 460 | 650 | 880 | 1,000 |
| **Black or Black British** | | | | | |
| Caribbean | 1,600 | 1,700 | 1,600 | 1,600 | 1,600 |
| African | 1,800 | 2,300 | 2,400 | 2,400 | 2,300 |
| Any other Black background | 870 | 880 | 900 | 900 | 880 |
| **Other ethnic groups** | | | | | |
| Chinese | 80 | 120 | 120 | 120 | 130 |
| Any other ethnic group | 750 | 840 | 900 | 1,000 | 1,200 |

SOURCE: Children looked after in England (including adoption and care leavers), year ending 31 March 2007, DfES.

Figures from Scotland and Wales are illustrated in **Charts 1.19** and **1.20**. From these charts it can be seen that the numbers have been rising over the last few years in much the same way as in England. The age distribution of children and young people looked after in England in 2007 is shown in **Chart 1.21**. From this it can be seen that by far the greatest number is to be found among the 10-15 year-olds. However, again, this is based on a snapshot of the population and masks the rapid throughput amongst the younger age groups.

We now turn to some of the evidence showing the disadvantages suffered by those who are looked after in England. Figures in **Chart 1.22** illustrate the proportions of looked after young people achieving educational qualifications. From this it can be seen that, although there has been some small increase

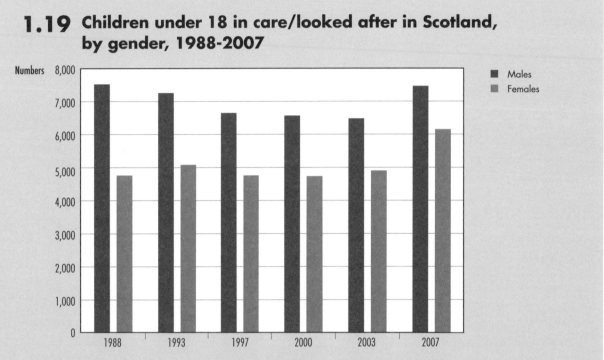

**1.19 Children under 18 in care/looked after in Scotland, by gender, 1988-2007**

SOURCE: Scottish Government. Health and Care Series: Children Looked After Statistics, 2007.

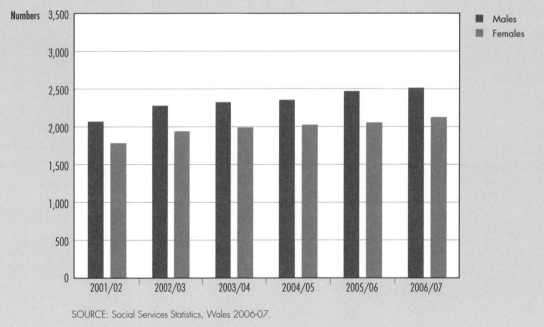

**1.20 Children in care/looked after in Wales, by gender, 2001/02-2006/07**

SOURCE: Social Services Statistics, Wales 2006-07.

## 1.21 Children and young people in care/looked after in England, by age, 2007

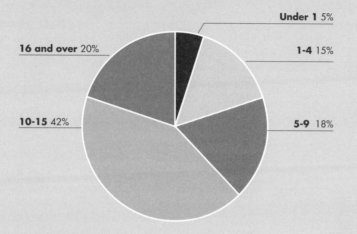

Under 1 5%

1-4 15%

16 and over 20%

10-15 42%

5-9 18%

SOURCE: Children looked after in England (including adoption and care leavers), year ending 31 March 2007, SFR, DfES.

## 1.22 Proportion of young people in care achieving 1 or more GCSEs/GNVQs at grades A-C, in England, 1999/00-2005/06

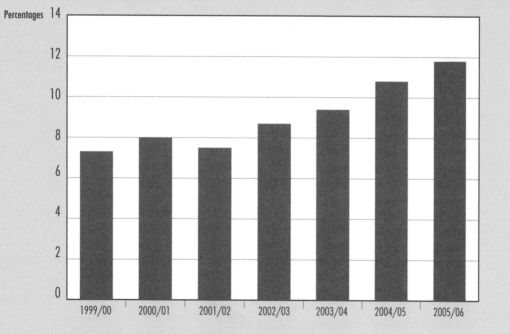

SOURCE: Outcome Indicator returns based on year ending 30 September, DCSF.

over the years since 1999, there still remain less than 12% of this group attaining even the minimum educational qualification. Figures shown in **Chart 1.23** demonstrate a significant increase over five years for those in education, employment or training at age 19, but in 2006, 30% are still outside the education, employment and training arena. Finally, figures illustrated in **Chart 1.24** tell us that while, in 2006, only 2% of all young people in their last year of compulsory education have no educational qualifications, for the looked after population this figure was 37% in the same year. Again this represents some improvement since the year 2000 but still reflects an enormous disparity in levels of achievement.

## 1.23 Proportion of care leavers at age 19 by activity, in England, 2002-2006

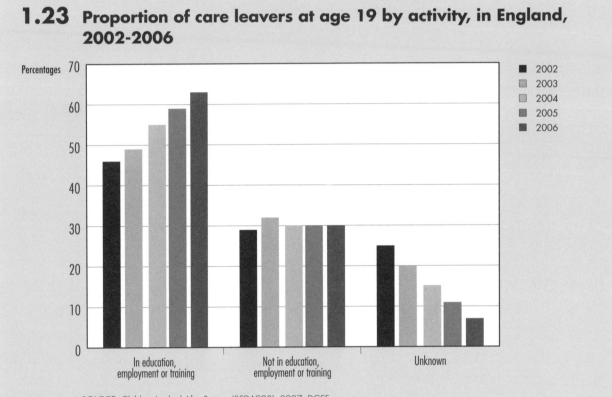

SOURCE: Children Looked After Returns (SSDA903), 2007, DCSF.

## 1.24 Pupils in their last year of compulsory education with no GCSEs or equivalent, 2000-2006

| Year | All children | Looked after children |
|------|--------------|-----------------------|
| 2000 | 6% | 51% |
| 2001 | 6% | 50% |
| 2002 | 5% | 47% |
| 2003 | 5% | 47% |
| 2004 | 4% | 44% |
| 2005 | 4% | 40% |
| 2006 | 2% | 37% |

SOURCE: Children Looked After Returns (SSDA903), 2007, DCSF.

## 1.25 Children and young people in care/looked after in England, by placement, 2006

Numbers

| Placement | All children | 10-15 | 16 and over |
|---|---|---|---|
| Foster placements | 42,000 | 19,100 | 5,700 |
| Placed for adoption | 2,900 | 170 | 10 |
| Placement with parents | 5,300 | 1,900 | 800 |
| Other placements in the community | 1,600 | 50 | 1,500 |
| Secure units, homes and hostels | 6,600 | 3,800 | 2,700 |
| Other residential settings | 600 | 220 | 230 |
| Residential schools | 1,100 | 750 | 320 |
| **All children** | **60,300** | **26,100** | **11,300** |

SOURCE: Children looked after by local authorities, year ending 31 March 2006, DFES.

## 1.26 Applications for asylum in the UK from unaccompanied children, by age, 2006

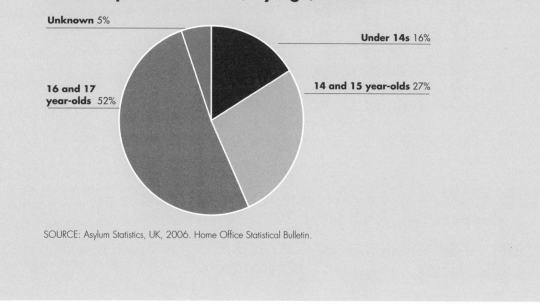

Unknown 5%

Under 14s 16%

16 and 17 year-olds 52%

14 and 15 year-olds 27%

SOURCE: Asylum Statistics, UK, 2006. Home Office Statistical Bulletin.

To conclude this section on the looked after population, it is also of importance to see how placements are distributed among different types of care. Figures in **Chart 1.25** illustrate the placements for all age groups and, in particular, for the adolescent population it can be seen that significant proportions are in residential and secure accommodation.

Turning now to asylum seekers, figures illustrated in **Chart 1.26** indicate that among the under-18s the highest numbers are among the 16 and 17 year-olds,

as might be expected. **Chart 1.27** illustrates all ages and shows gender differences. Here it can be seen that among young men the highest numbers are among the 15-19 year-olds. However, among young women the greatest numbers are among an older group, the 22-25 year-olds. Lastly, we can look in **Chart 1.28** at how the numbers of asylum seekers have changed over the period from 1997 to 2006. It is striking to see that applications reached a high point in 2002, but have fallen very sharply since then.

## 1.27 Applications for asylum in the UK, by gender and age, 2006

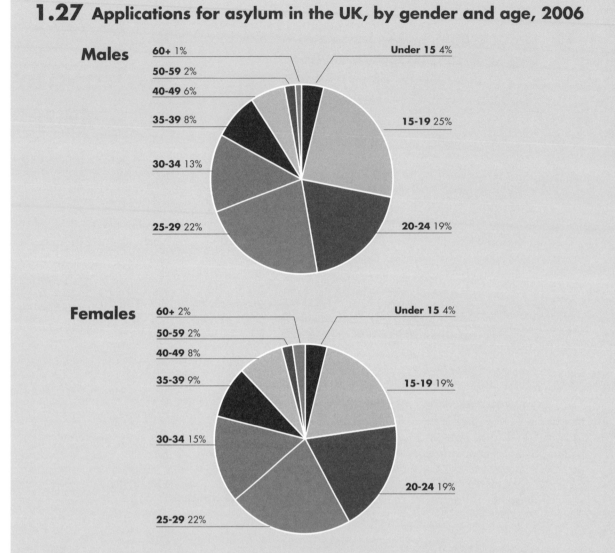

**Males**

60+ 1%
50-59 2%
40-49 6%
35-39 8%
30-34 13%
25-29 22%
Under 15 4%
15-19 25%
20-24 19%

**Females**

60+ 2%
50-59 2%
40-49 8%
35-39 9%
30-34 15%
25-29 22%
Under 15 4%
15-19 19%
20-24 19%

SOURCE: Asylum Statistics UK, 2006. Home Office Statistical Bulletin.

## 1.28 Applications for asylum in the UK, by location of application, 1997-2006

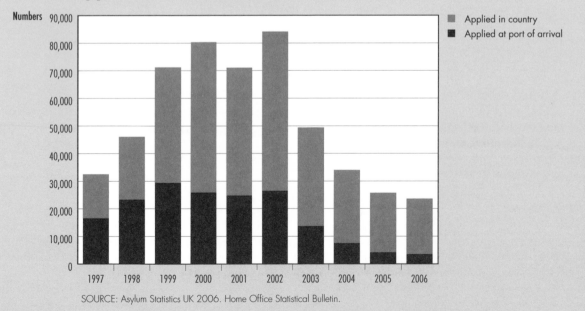

Numbers

- Applied in country
- Applied at port of arrival

SOURCE: Asylum Statistics UK 2006. Home Office Statistical Bulletin.

# CHAPTER

## Education, Training and Employment

# 2

**KEY MESSAGES**

## Improving performance in GCSEs

Performance at GCSE level continues to improve. In 2007, nearly 66% of young women and 58% of young men in England obtained at least 5 GCSEs at grades A-C (Chart 2.1)

## Varying attainment levels

There is substantial variation in educational performance between young people in different ethnic groups. The highest levels of attainment are achieved by young Chinese women, 85% of whom obtain 5 GCSEs at grades A-C compared to only 62% of White British females (Chart 2.4)

## High levels of scientific literacy

Comparative European figures indicate that British young people do particularly well in scientific literacy, coming equal first with their German counterparts among OECD countries (Chart 2.11)

## Nearly 10% are NEET

In 2007, around 180,000 young people aged 16-18 were not in education, employment or training. Although the numbers who are NEET have fallen quite sharply since the 2005 peak, the overall total is still higher than it was in 2001 (Chart 2.13)

## Rising unemployment

After more than ten years of reductions, the unemployment rate among 16-24 year olds in the UK has risen quite substantially since 2004 (Chart 2.18)

# Education, Training and Employment

The world of education has seen rapid changes in the last few years. The growth of the academy programme and the increasing diversity of types of secondary schools is but one element in a rapidly shifting landscape. The 14-19 Education and Skills Bill currently before Parliament includes a commitment to the raising of the school leaving age to 17 by 2013, and to 18 by 2015. In addition to this, there is a move to introduce Diplomas and a Foundation Learning Tier, as well as to increase substantially the Apprenticeship programme. At the time of writing, the Government has also made a commitment to making PSHE (Personal, Social and Health Education, including Sex and Relationships Education) compulsory throughout the four key stages of primary and secondary education. This is a huge step forward and has been widely welcomed in most quarters. Finally, the secondary curriculum is currently subject to review and it may be that more substantive change is on the way.

The first topic we will consider in this chapter is that of GCSE performance. Figures in **Chart 2.1** show a marked increase in the numbers of pupils obtaining five or more GCSEs in the period 1980/81 to 2006/07. Over this period, the number of young people in the UK obtaining five or more A-C grades at GCSE has increased nearly threefold. This is true for both boys and girls, although in an absolute sense girls outperform boys at this age.

The year on year improvement in the number of boys and girls achieving five or more passes at A-C grades clearly reflects the increasing emphasis on the importance of examinations. However, it should be noted that there is a continuing problem in distinguishing between genuinely improved academic performance and the possibility of altered criteria for the marking of examinations. A further possible reason for improved performance is that the nature of the teaching to GCSE level has also changed over the last decades. A greater reliance on course-work, greater use of new technologies and more informal approaches to learning may also be having an impact on levels of performance.

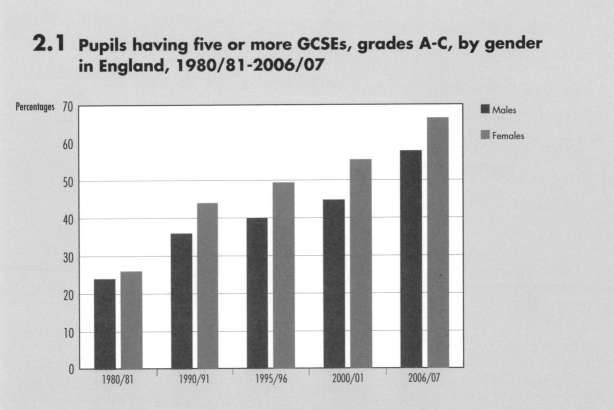

## 2.1  Pupils having five or more GCSEs, grades A-C, by gender in England, 1980/81-2006/07

Percentages

■ Males
■ Females

SOURCE: GCSE and Equivalent Results in England 2006/07 (Revised). SFR01/2008, DCSF.

## 2.2 Pupils having five or more GCSEs, grades A-C, by gender in the four countries of the UK, 2005/06

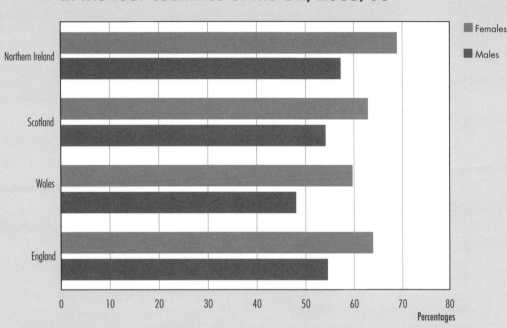

SOURCE: Department for Children, Schools and Families; Welsh Assembly; Scottish Govt; and Northern Ireland Dept. of Education, 2007.

## 2.3 Pupils having five or more GCSEs, grades A-C, by regions of England, 2006/07

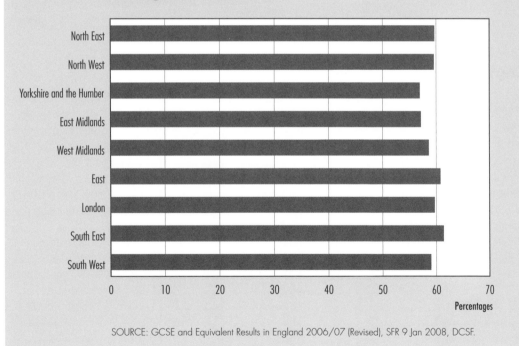

SOURCE: GCSE and Equivalent Results in England 2006/07 (Revised), SFR 9 Jan 2008, DCSF.

In **Chart 2.2**, comparisons are drawn between the four countries of the UK. It is evident that performance is better in Northern Ireland than it is in the other three countries. In the past, Scotland was very similar to Northern Ireland but the most recent figures show England and Scotland at much the same level of achievement. Figures in **Chart 2.3** illustrate regional variations within England, showing higher levels of attainment in the East and South East and lower levels in Yorkshire and the Humber and in the East Midlands.

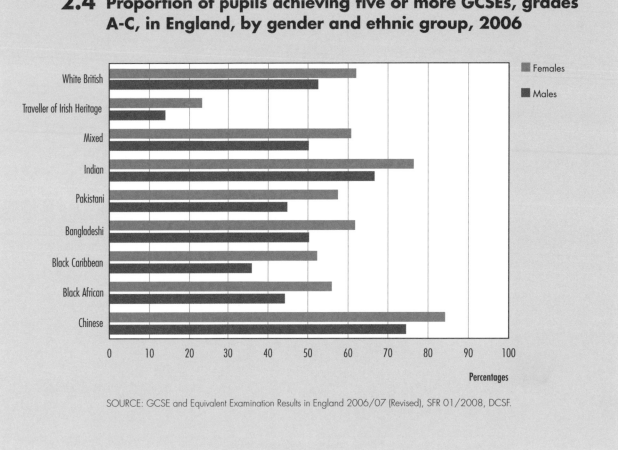

**2.4** **Proportion of pupils achieving five or more GCSEs, grades A-C, in England, by gender and ethnic group, 2006**

SOURCE: GCSE and Equivalent Examination Results in England 2006/07 (Revised), SFR 01/2008, DCSF.

One key issue in looking at educational performance has to do with ethnicity and, as might be expected, there is marked variation in attainment among ethnic groups in the UK. This is reflected in the data shown in **Chart 2.4**. From these figures it can be seen that young people from Indian and Chinese backgrounds attain higher levels of achievement than those from other backgrounds. Those from Black Caribbean and Pakistani backgrounds perform least well, apart from those from traveller backgrounds. As can be seen, this group has an especially poor achievement record, something that should be of considerable concern to policy makers.

Turning now to A levels, figures in **Chart 2.5** show that the increase in those achieving one or more A levels was most marked between 1997 and 2002. From then onwards the trend has levelled off, with much the same numbers achieving A level passes between 2002 and 2007. As we have noted, new qualifications are being introduced and, as can be seen from **Chart 2.6**, there is an increasing number of young people taking the NVQ and SVQ (National Vocational Qualification and Scottish Vocational Qualification). This chart shows the increase between 1994/95 to 2006/07, whilst figures in **Chart 2.7** show the sector in which these qualifications are being obtained. As can be seen, health, public service and care, together with retail and commercial are the two most popular areas.

## 2.5 17 year-olds achieving 1 or more, or 3 or more GCE A level passes, in England, 1994-2007

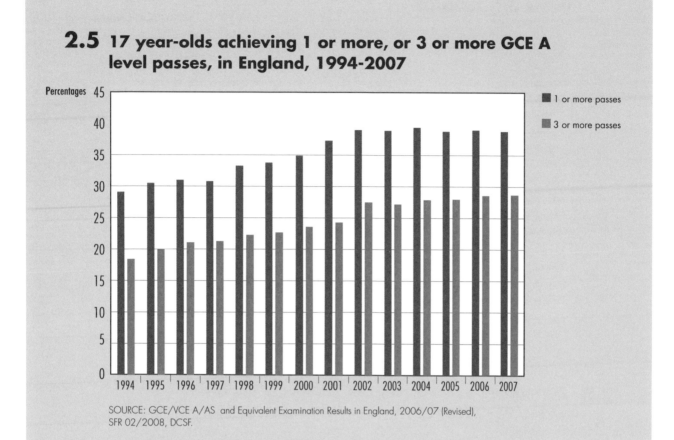

Percentages

■ 1 or more passes
■ 3 or more passes

SOURCE: GCE/VCE A/AS and Equivalent Examination Results in England, 2006/07 (Revised), SFR 02/2008, DCSF.

## 2.6 Total numbers of young people achieving NVQs/SVQs in the UK, 1994/95-2006/07

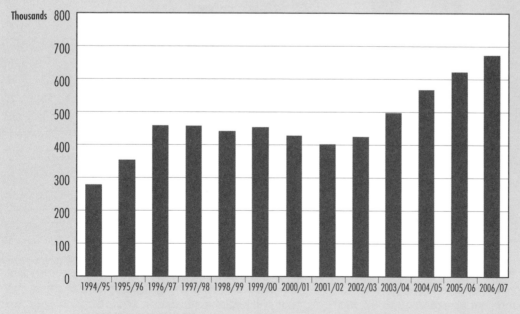

Thousands

SOURCE: NISVQ/QCA, 2008.

Turning now to a very different aspect of school performance, as a result of research produced by the OECD, it is possible to compare educational attainments among 15 year-olds in different European countries. As part of the Programme for International Student Assessment (PISA), over a quarter of a million pupils in 32 countries were first surveyed in 2000, and then again in 2003 and 2006. Some of the findings from the 2006 survey are illustrated in **Chart 2.11**. As

can be seen, British pupils are certainly doing as well as those from our main European competitors and, in 2006, they did particularly well in scientific literacy compared with the OECD average. These are useful findings, especially when so much of the rhetoric about British young people tends to concentrate on the negative rather than on the positive achievements of this age group.

## 2.11 Student performance on combined reading, scientific and mathematical literacy scales, for selected OECD countries, by gender, 2006

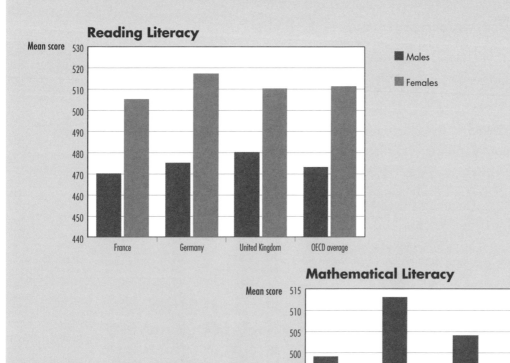

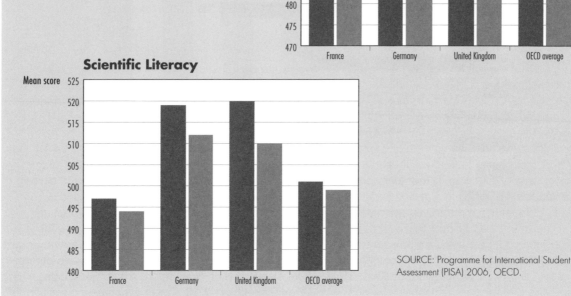

SOURCE: Programme for International Student Assessment (PISA) 2006, OECD.

## 2.12 Young people aged 16-18 in education and training in England, by gender, 1985-2007

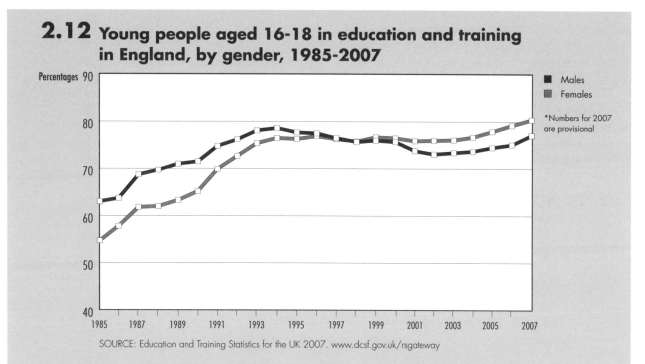

■ Males
■ Females

*Numbers for 2007 are provisional

SOURCE: Education and Training Statistics for the UK 2007. www.dcsf.gov.uk/rsgateway

## 2.13 Numbers 16-18 year-olds classed as NEET (not in education, employment or training) in England, 1996-2007

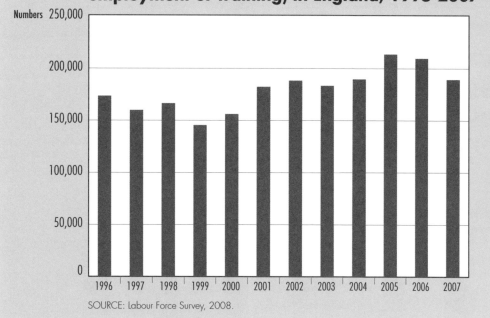

SOURCE: Labour Force Survey, 2008.

In previous editions of this publication, we have repeatedly referred to the fact that a key change for young people over the past twenty years has been the increased numbers staying on in education and training post-16. This shift is illustrated well in **Chart 2.12** but it can be seen here that the major change occurred between 1985 and the early 1990s, rather than in the 21st century. In essence, the numbers remaining in education and training have stayed fairly constant since 1993, although there has been some variation over the years. It does look now as if between 2005 and 2007 there has been a clear upward trend, with the total in 2007 reaching nearly 79% of this age group. We have noted the commitment of the Government to the raising of the school leaving age

over the next decade, and so it is important to note how large the shift will have to be to ensure participation in education for the total 16-18 year age group.

Another aspect of the picture relating to the 16-18 year age group has been a question of how many of this group could be classified as NEET (not in education, employment or training). This is a difficult and unpopular term, as well as being a complex issue since there are a variety of reasons why young people remain outside the education and training arena. Some are at home having caring responsibilities and others are disaffected or excluded from the mainstream. Figures in **Chart 2.13** show the numbers classified as

NEET over a ten year period and, in spite of numerous Government initiatives, it is clear that the numbers remain stubbornly high. According to the DCSF in 2006, 10.4% of the 16-18 year age group were classified as NEET, whilst in 2007 the number had dropped to 9.4%. As can be seen in **Chart 2.13** there does appear to have been a drop in numbers since 2005 but this has to be set against a general trend over the decade.

Turning now to those over 18, evidence from the OECD makes it possible to compare the number of students engaged in post-18 education in different European countries. Data illustrated in **Chart 2.14** shows the UK lagging a long way behind other countries. It is clear that there are very different cultures across Europe, with many countries encouraging 80% or even in some cases 90% of young people to continue in higher education post-18. In the UK, only 48% continue in education after their 18th birthday.

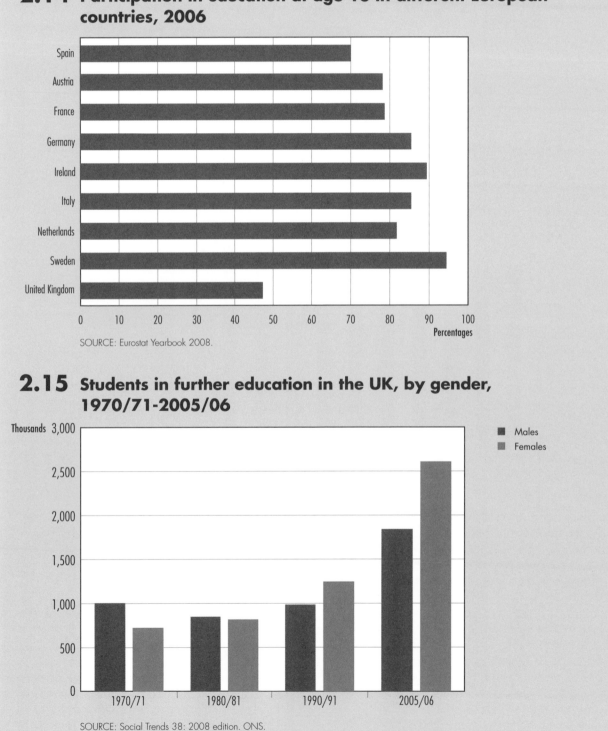

**2.14** **Participation in education at age 18 in different European countries, 2006**

SOURCE: Eurostat Yearbook 2008.

**2.15** **Students in further education in the UK, by gender, 1970/71-2005/06**

SOURCE: Social Trends 38: 2008 edition. ONS.

We have noted the trend towards increased participation, and this can be seen in both further and higher education. Comparisons across time are set out for further education in **Chart 2.15** and for higher education in **Chart 2.16**. These trends illustrate the extent of the changes that have occurred in the UK over recent years, most especially for young women. It is truly remarkable to note the historical shift, and to see how the numbers of young women have overtaken the numbers of young men in both further and higher education.

Figures in **Chart 2.17** illustrate the numbers in higher education coming from minority backgrounds. As can be seen the group having the highest number in this sector is the Asian Indian group, followed by the Black African group. Most other minority groups have a much lower take-up of higher education, and it would be good to see this altered. Of particular note is the Chinese group, who do so well at the GCSE level (see Chart 2.4) and yet do not appear to continue high levels of achievement post-18.

**2.16** **Students in higher education in the UK, by gender, 1970/71-2005/06**

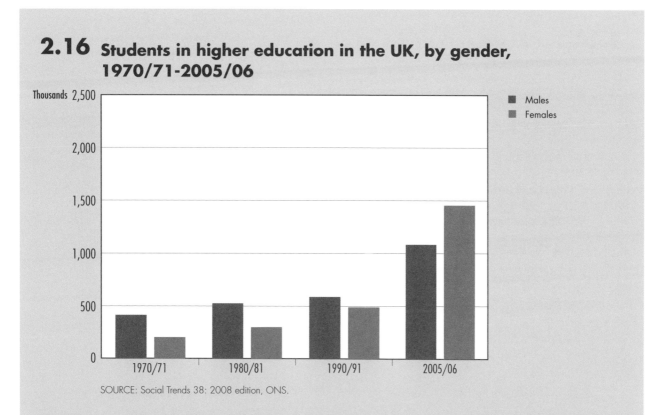

SOURCE: Social Trends 38: 2008 edition, ONS.

**2.17** **Ethnic minority students in higher education, as a percentage of all applicants accepted through UCAS, in the UK, 2006/07**

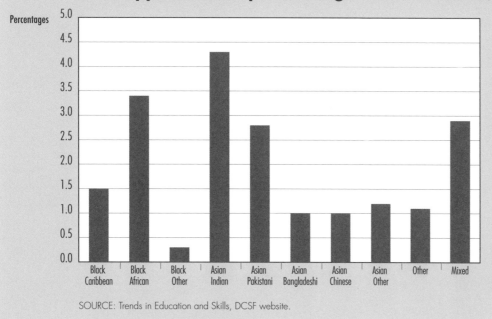

SOURCE: Trends in Education and Skills, DCSF website.

# Employment

Changes in the labour market over the past 20 years have been profound, and have impacted on young people just as much as on other sectors of the population. As we have noted, more and more young people are remaining in education or training, and more and more are continuing into higher education post-18. As a result, entry into the labour market is delayed, and the consequences of this delay have been well charted by Liza Catan's major research programme, entitled "Youth, citizenship and social change" (Catan, 2002). One feature of the labour market is, of course, the numbers not able to get work at all, and figures in **Chart 2.18** show a worsening picture for young people from 2005 onwards. Indeed, as we write, the outcome of the global financial crisis is unclear, but of one thing we can be certain, that amongst all groups of workers, those between the ages of 16 and 24 will be the worst off.

As far as regional trends are concerned, it can be seen from figures in **Chart 2.19** that there is wide variation between different parts of the country in rates of unemployment. Among UK countries, rates are highest in Scotland, and they are higher in London and in the West Midlands than in other regions of England. Finally, we look at European comparisons of unemployment rates for those below the age of 25. Figures in **Chart 2.20** show that the UK is broadly in the middle range in respect of such rates, although due to widely different employment circumstances in different countries, these figures need to be treated with caution.

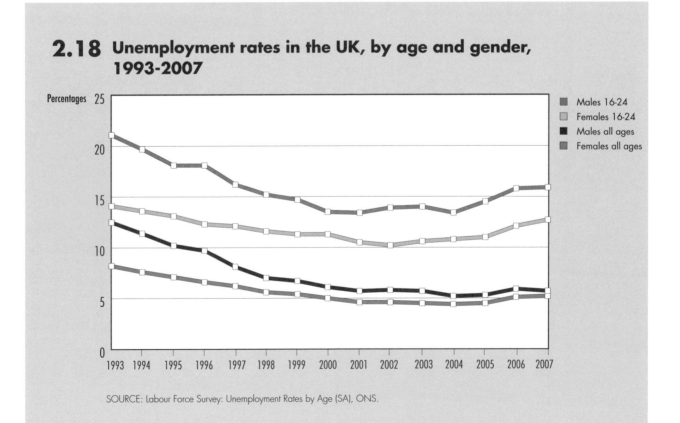

**2.18** **Unemployment rates in the UK, by age and gender, 1993-2007**

Legend:
- Males 16-24
- Females 16-24
- Males all ages
- Females all ages

SOURCE: Labour Force Survey: Unemployment Rates by Age (SA), ONS.

## 2.19 Unemployment rates for 16-24 year-olds, by country and region in the UK, spring 2007

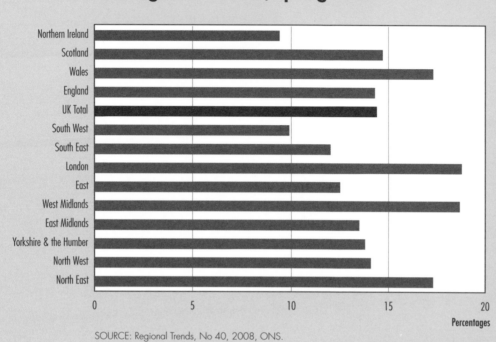

SOURCE: Regional Trends, No 40, 2008, ONS.

## 2.20 Unemployment rates of population aged less than 25 years in selected EU countries, 2007

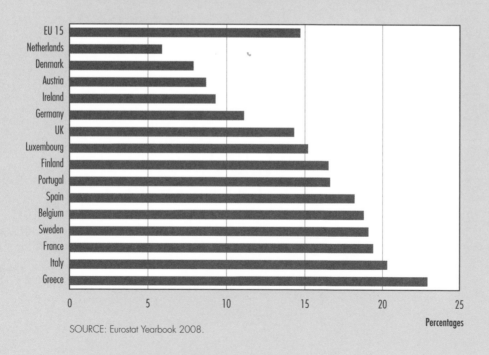

SOURCE: Eurostat Yearbook 2008.

# References

Catan L (2002) *Youth, Citizenship and Social Change*. Trust for the Study of Adolescence. Brighton.

# CHAPTER 3

## Primary Health Care and Health Behaviours

## Decrease in obesity

Following steady increases over the previous ten years, the prevalence of obesity has decreased since 2004 to 17.1% in girls and 17.6% in boys by 2006 (Chart 3.7)

## Increased healthy eating

Between 2002 and 2006, the proportion of English 15 year-olds who ate fruit daily increased from 22% to 33% for boys, and from 28% to 44% for girls. However, young people in Scotland and Wales are less likely to eat fruit every day than their English counterparts (Chart 3.10)

## Fewer regular smokers

In 2007, 19% of girls and 12% of boys were regular smokers by age 15. This represents a marked reduction over the previous two years from the 2005 rates of 25% and 16% for 15 year-old girls and boys respectively (Chart 3.12)

## Rise in teenage drinking

There has been a dramatic doubling in the amount of alcohol consumed by 11-15 year olds since 1990. Early drunkenness in England, Scotland and Wales at or before the age of 13 is among the highest reported for any countries in the European Union (Charts 3.19 and 3.21)

## Concern for the health of girls

The health of girls in relation to risk behaviours and experience of primary health care services warrants focused attention. It is notable that girls have relatively high rates of smoking and drinking and lower rates of protective behaviours such as physical activity.

# Primary Health Care

Adolescence represents a critical time for the health and well-being of an individual. The transition to adulthood provides numerous physical and emotional challenges and the pattern for many future health-related behaviours may be set during the teenage years.

Despite young people having less morbidity relative to other age groups, there has been an increasing awareness that the health of young people actually represents a very complex picture. This picture is shaped by health behaviours and the impact of chronic and long term conditions, as well as being mediated by social inequalities, such as growing up in poverty. Responding to the health needs of young people, decreasing risk and increasing resilience are consequently perceived as significant challenges for public health (Hawkins et al.,1999). It is therefore not surprising that, the Chief Medical Officer's Annual Report for 2007 (Donaldson, 2008) in drawing attention to major health challenges, called for a new focus on teenage health and specifically called for services to be more responsive to the particular needs of young people.

In the UK, health policies have attempted to address not only the health protection needs of children, but have also sought to deliver health promotion strategies that ensure and enhance the safety, achievement and well-being of young people and their families. In particular, the identification of ways to increase and sustain health-promoting behaviours among young people has in recent years represented a priority for UK health promotion and policy-led interventions. For example, the National Healthy Schools Programme was established in 1999 as a joint Department of Health (DH) and Department for Children, Schools and Families (DCSF) initiative.

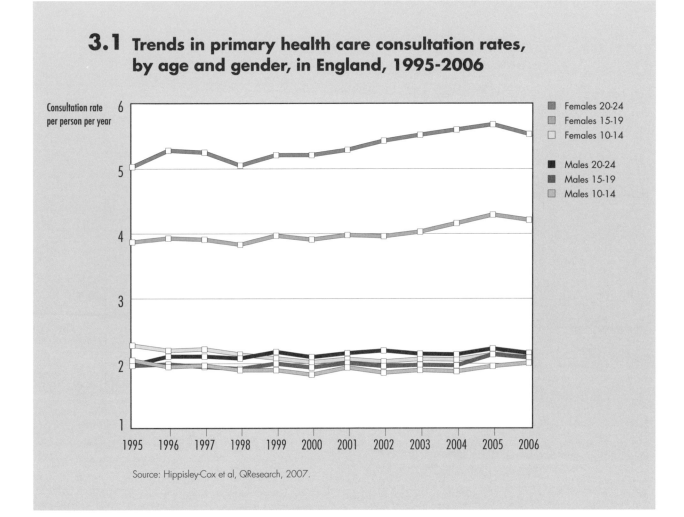

**3.1 Trends in primary health care consultation rates, by age and gender, in England, 1995-2006**

Source: Hippisley-Cox et al, QResearch, 2007.

This chapter commences with a consideration of young people's usage and experience of primary health care (PHC) and particularly general practice. Drawing on the QResearch database derived from anonymised health records, Hippisley-Cox et al. (2007) looked at the trends in consultation rates for general practice. Data presented in **Chart 3.1** illustrate a relatively stable rate of consultation by young people over the decade (with a small upward trend from 2004), as well as a consistent gender-based pattern of general practice usage. While male consultation patterns across adolescence remain relatively constant at about 2 consultations per year, for young women, late adolescence (15-19) marks a dramatic increase in consultation rates to about 4 consultations per year, with a further increase to just over 5 consultations per year by age 20-24 years.

Turning to young people's reasons for consultation, Churchill et al.'s 2000 study remains the most detailed exploration of young peoples' experience of consultation with a general practitioner. Drawing on questionnaires and case note analysis, this shows in **Chart 3.2** that respiratory conditions (35%) and dermatological problems (29%) represented the most common reasons for young people to see their GP, a finding that illustrates the significance of asthma as a health issue for young people (see chapter 4).

**Chart 3.3** reports on teenagers' perspectives on their experience of talking to their GP from Balding's (2007) questionnaire study. This survey found that up to 23% of girls reported feeling 'quite' or 'very uneasy' with their doctor on their last visit. A finding that was echoed by the earlier Churchill study, which reported that 47% of girls agreed that they might not be able to talk to a doctor due to potential embarrassment compared to 39% of boys.

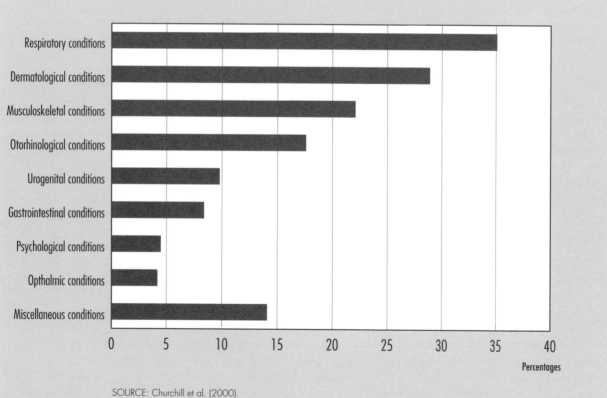

**3.2 Reasons for consultation with a GP, over a twelve month period**

SOURCE: Churchill et al. (2000).

**3.3** Talking to the doctor: *"Did young people feel at ease with the GP at their last visit?",* by age and gender

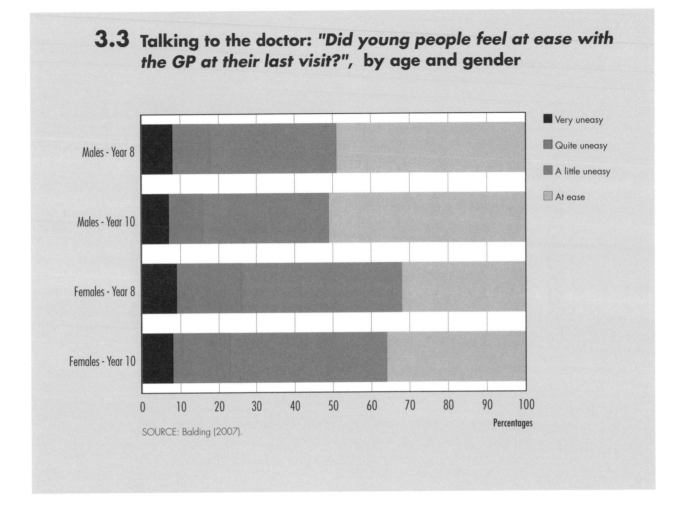

SOURCE: Balding (2007).

Overall, there is a notable dearth of up-to-date information relating to key areas of young people's usage of primary health care services. Further research is especially needed in relation to young people's experiences of the character and quality of primary health care. Condition-specific research would also be valuable in terms of understanding how to meet young people's needs including, for example, work on the response of PHC services to asthma and respiratory conditions among young people. Modern primary health care services encompass more than just 'the GP'. However, comparative research that considers teenagers' experiences of other members of the PHC team (such as practice nurses) is also notably absent from the current evidence base. Finally, the gendered consultation patterns warrant further examination of young women's experiences, particularly in terms of understanding how to ensure girls feel comfortable and positive about their encounters with general practice.

Turning from PHC service usage to consideration of broader health promotion and public health issues, the remainder of the chapter considers issues concerned with obesity and physical activity, substance use (including smoking and alcohol), and finally explores young people's perspectives on sources of health promotion support and advice.

Active lifestyles offer an array of potential positive health and social benefits for young people (Brooks and Magnusson, 2006). Declining rates of physical activity among young people and the linked issue of increasing obesity have both received considerable public attention in recent years. Current UK policy guidelines recommend 1 hour of moderate physical activity per day for children and young people. The Health Survey for England 2006 reported in detail on physical activity among young people. **Chart 3.4** details the proportion of young people in the survey achieving the recommended physical activity levels (identified as 'high' in the chart). The proportion of both sexes achieving the physical activity recommendation has remained relatively similar between the survey dates of 2002 and 2006. This consistency across the survey dates is also true for the gender difference in levels of activity. Indeed, it can be seen from the chart that the percentage of girls reporting high levels of physical activity is consistently lower than for boys across all age groups. In addition, the numbers of girls reporting high levels of physical activity significantly declines in later adolescence.

**Chart 3.5** considers the forms of physical activity participation among young people and offers further insight into the gendered character of physical activity rates. Sports and exercise were defined as including

## 3.4 Physical activity levels by age and gender (ages 10-15), in England, 2006

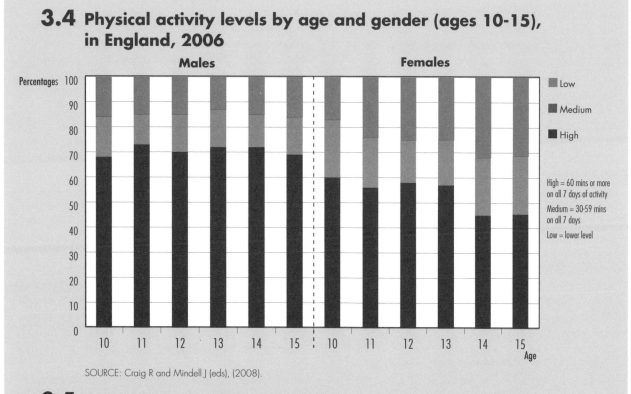

SOURCE: Craig R and Mindell J (eds), (2008).

## 3.5 Participation in different activities at ages 10 and 15, by gender, in England, 2006

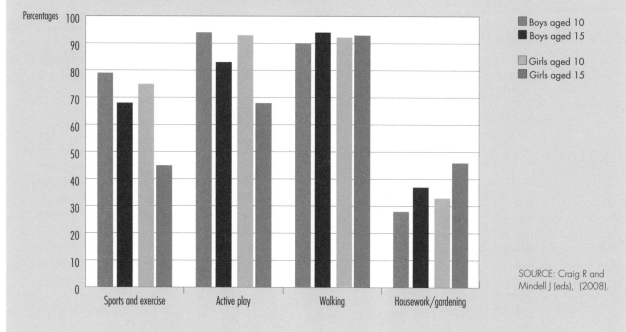

SOURCE: Craig R and Mindell J (eds), (2008).

organised and structured activities such as football or gymnastics, whereas active play included activities such as 'running about', riding a bike or playing active games. During middle childhood, rates of participation in sport, exercise and active play for both sexes is over 70%. However, a marked gender distinction becomes apparent by age 15. Although there is a drop in participation in sports and active play across all 15 year-olds, for girls participation in sport and exercise drops, for example, from 75% at age 10 to 45% at age 15, compared to a drop from 79% to 68% among boys. The cause of such a gender difference is complex, however the character of sports and exercise provision available for girls warrants examination. The chart also illustrates the contribution of walking to sustaining young people's physical activity rates, thereby supporting initiatives such as 'walk to school' campaigns. It also illustrates the importance of young people feeling comfortable and safe about walking in their local communities.

The UK government has implemented a public service agreement (PSA) to enhance the take up of sporting opportunities by 5 to 16 year-olds, by increasing the percentage of school children who spend a minimum of two hours each week on high quality physical education (PE) and school sport, within and beyond the curriculum, from 25% in 2002 to 75% by 2006 and to 85% by 2008. **Chart 3.6** shows a steady increase since 2004/05 in PE participation across year groups among the 21,745 schools that took part in the Schools Sports Survey (Craig and Mindell, 2008). Among years 7-9 the target of over 75% participation in quality PE and out of hours school sport was clearly met by 2006. The decline in participation in school-based activity among years 10 and 11 coincides with the commencement of study for GCSE and other national examinations.

Rising levels of obesity and young people who are overweight have led to considerable concern among both the public and policymakers in recent years. In policy terms, obesity in childhood has been addressed through a number of policy developments such as healthy eating initiatives established via the healthy schools programme. These are linked to achieving the PSA target of reducing the number of obese and overweight children to 2000 levels by 2020. In 2006, 16% of children aged 2 to 15 were classed as obese,

representing an overall increase from 11% in 1995 (Information Centre, 2008). **Chart 3.7** provides an overview of the rise in obesity levels among 11-15 year-olds since 1995. Despite the overall increase since 1995, the prevalence of obesity has fallen since 2004. Although future data will determine if this is part of a downward trend, it may be that the decrease in the percentage of young people who are being identified as obese is an indication of positive impacts of public health and health promotion policy in this area.

Health-related attitudes and behaviours of young people in relation to body size, weight maintenance and nutrition are the focus of charts 3.8-3.11. **Chart 3.8** presents findings from Balding's 2007 survey. This highlights that a consistently higher proportion of girls compared to boys would like to lose weight, a disparity that also increases with age, so that while 42% of year 6 girls would like to lose weight compared to 31% of boys, only 28% of year 10 boys would like to do so compared to 57% of year 10 girls. Moreover, the Balding study (2007) also identified that, of the year 10 females wanting to lose weight, the majority were of healthy weight and some could be considered to be underweight. International comparison from the HBSC study (Currie et al., 2008) indicates wide disparities across countries and, significantly, the countries within

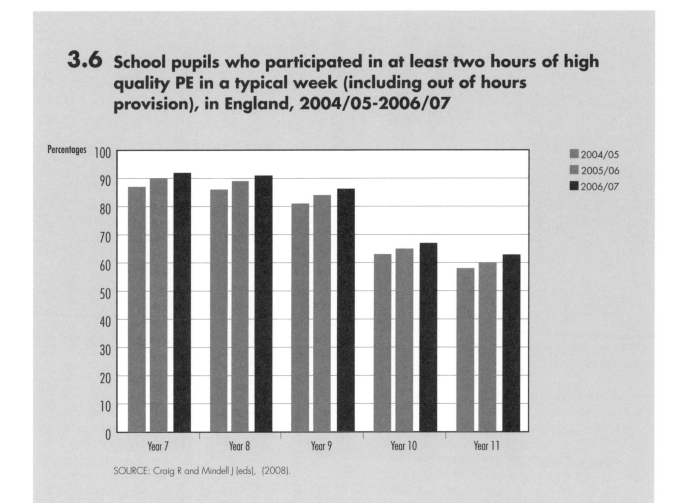

**3.6** **School pupils who participated in at least two hours of high quality PE in a typical week (including out of hours provision), in England, 2004/05-2006/07**

SOURCE: Craig R and Mindell J (eds), (2008).

## 3.7 Obesity prevalence among 11-15 year-olds, by gender, in England, 1995-2006

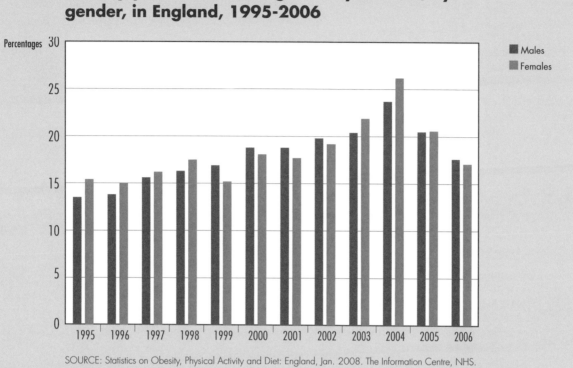

SOURCE: Statistics on Obesity, Physical Activity and Diet: England, Jan. 2008. The Information Centre, NHS.

## 3.8 Attitudes to weight by gender and school year, in England, 2007

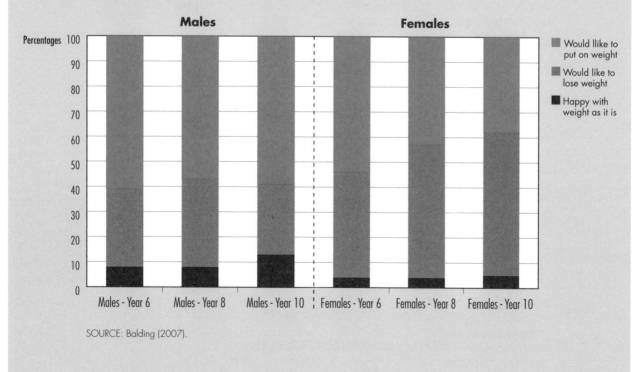

SOURCE: Balding (2007).

the UK in terms of the proportions of young people engaged in dieting and weight control behaviours (**Chart 3.9**). Dieting as a weight control strategy may be problematic for young people, leading to starve and binge cycles, which may increase weight in the long term or have negative developmental consequences. The HBSC study identifies that by age 15, across all countries, girls are much more likely to be engaging in dieting than their male peers. In fact, the proportion of boys engaging in weight reduction actually decreases with age. **Chart 3.9** also indicates that higher proportions of young people from Wales and Scotland report that they are dieting than 11 and 15 year-olds in England. The reasons for such disparity within the UK remain unclear. How they may be related to relative affluence, different food cultures, levels of self-esteem or potentially different health promotion strategies towards dieting and healthy eating in each country raise important questions for further research.

In recent years, achieving an improvement in healthy eating among young people has been a UK-wide Government strategy with a number of schools-based healthy eating initiatives. Considering specific types of food eaten can be a useful indication of the character of young people's diets and food consumption.

## 3.9 Proportion of 11 and 15 year-olds who had engaged in dieting and weight control behaviour, in selected countries, 2005/06

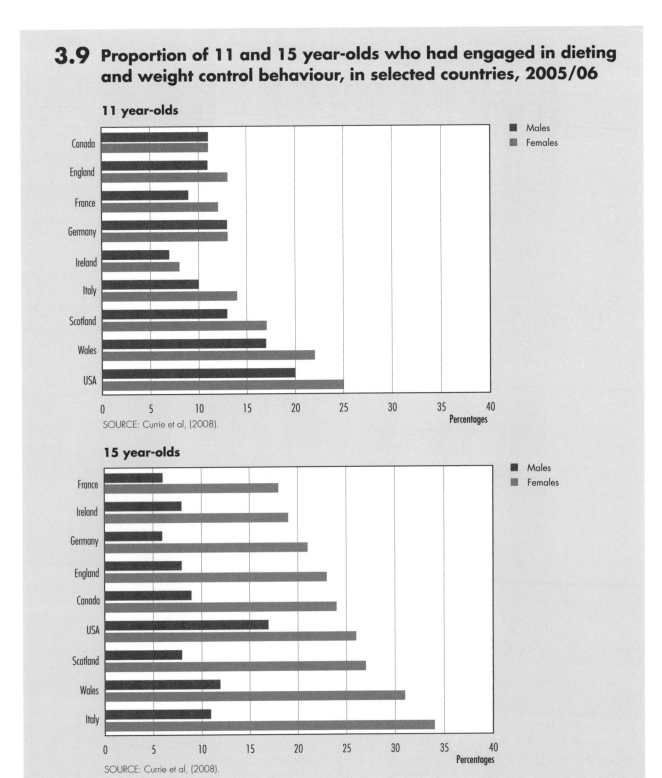

**11 year-olds**

SOURCE: Currie et al, (2008).

**15 year-olds**

SOURCE: Currie et al, (2008).

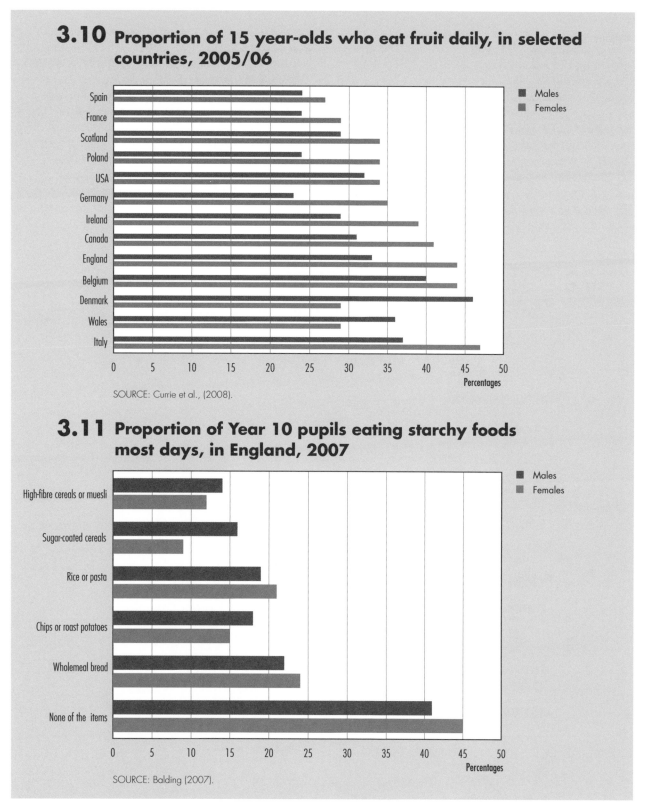

**3.10** **Proportion of 15 year-olds who eat fruit daily, in selected countries, 2005/06**

SOURCE: Currie et al., (2008).

**3.11** **Proportion of Year 10 pupils eating starchy foods most days, in England, 2007**

SOURCE: Balding (2007).

In 2002, the proportion of English 15 year-olds in the HBSC survey who ate fruit daily was 22% for boys and 28% for girls (Morgan et al., 2006). **Chart 3.10** shows that in 2006 daily fruit eating had increased to 33% for boys and 44% for girls (Currie et al., 2008). England now ranks third among all countries in the HBSC study for daily fruit eating.  Importantly, the 2006 HBSC survey data also highlight variations with the UK, with young people from both Scotland and Wales appearing to be less likely than their English counterparts to eat fruit every day. Balding (2007) considered the range of starchy foods eaten by young

people on 'most days'. Such foods are important components of an adolescent's diet as they can offer high nutritional content and low fat options (aside from chips). **Chart 3.11** presents data on these foods for year 10 pupils (14-15 year-olds), including high fibre options such as cereals and wholemeal bread. Balding (2007) reports a decline since 1990 in the consumption of chips and roast potatoes on most days to 18% for males and 15% for females. However, a high proportion of year 10 pupils (41% of males and 45% of females) report not consuming any high energy, starchy foods on a daily basis.

Young people's health and well being can be significantly affected by the degree of exposure to a range of health risk behaviours. This chapter now focuses attention on three key areas of risk behaviours, smoking, alcohol consumption and the use of illegal substances. Looking first at smoking, it is apparent from **Chart 3.12** that smoking increases markedly by age; in 2007, 19% of girls and 12% of boys were regular smokers by age 15. However, the 2007 rates represent a significant reduction in the proportions of young people smoking from the 2005 rates of 25% of 15 year-old girls and 16% of boys reported in the 6th Edition of Key Data in Adolescence (Coleman and Schofield, 2007). A detailed time-trend analysis is provided in **Chart 3.13** which shows that although smoking rates appeared to be stabilising since 2003, 2006 marked a reduction in smoking rates for both sexes to a 25-year low. Additional detail of smoking behaviour among 15 year-olds is given in **Chart 3.14**, which further demonstrates the gender disparity: more boys than girls have never smoked and more girls than boys are occasional and regular smokers. The distribution of 15 year-old smokers, occasional smokers and those who have never smoked has also remained relatively constant since 2005 (Coleman and Schofield, 2007).

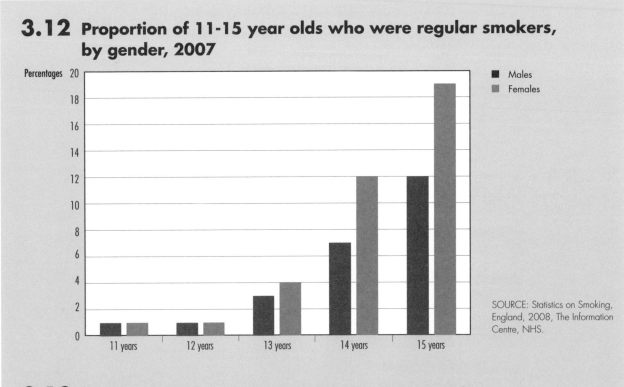

**3.12** **Proportion of 11-15 year olds who were regular smokers, by gender, 2007**

SOURCE: Statistics on Smoking, England, 2008, The Information Centre, NHS.

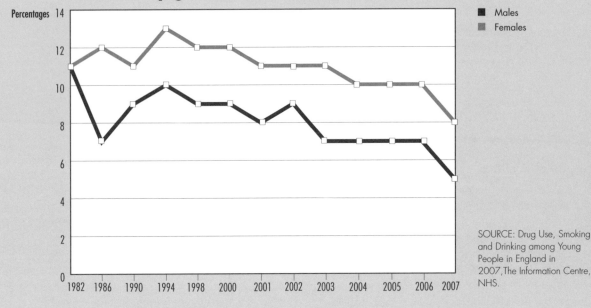

**3.13** **Proportion of 11-15 year-olds who were regular smokers, by gender, 1982-2007**

SOURCE: Drug Use, Smoking and Drinking among Young People in England in 2007, The Information Centre, NHS.

## 3.14 Smoking behaviour among 15 year-olds, by gender, in England, 2007

|  | Boys % | Girls % |
|---|---|---|
| Regular smoker | 12 | 19 |
| Occasional smoker | 8 | 13 |
| Used to smoke | 10 | 12 |
| Tried smoking | 20 | 18 |
| Never smoked | 50 | 39 |
| Ever smoked | 50 | 61 |

SOURCE: Statistics on Smoking, England, 2008, The Information Centre, NHS.

## 3.15 Proportion of 16-19 year-olds smoking in Britain, by gender, 1980-2006

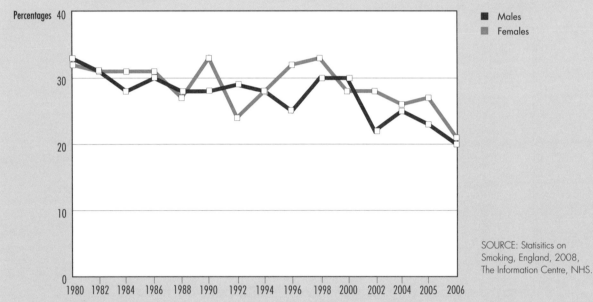

SOURCE: Statisitics on Smoking, England, 2008, The Information Centre, NHS.

## 3.16 Proportion of 20-24 year-olds smoking in Britain, by gender, 1980-2006

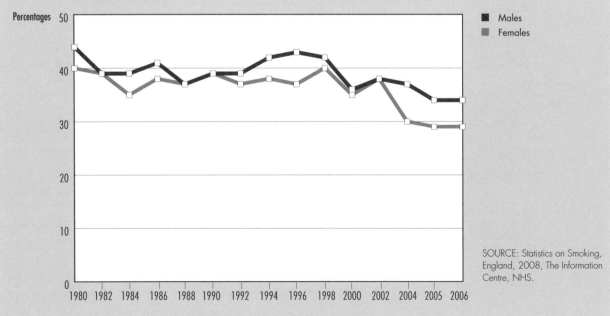

SOURCE: Statistics on Smoking, England, 2008, The Information Centre, NHS.

**Charts 3.15** and **3.16** illustrate the historical trends for smoking among 16-19 year-olds and 20-24 year-olds. In the post-16 groups there are greater similarities between young men and young women than in the younger groups. Among 16-19 year-olds in 2006, smoking prevalence among male and females approached parity, although a gender difference has continued among the older age group. International comparisons from the HBSC study (Currie et al., 2004, 2008) illustrate a general downward trend in regular weekly smoking across the majority of more economically developed countries, including England and the USA (**Chart 3.17**). Although importantly, in Scotland, the rates have remained relatively unchanged between the HBSC survey points of 2001/02 and 2005/06.

## 3.17 Proportion of 15 year-olds who reported smoking at least weekly, in selected countries, 2001/02 and 2005/06

|  | 2001/02 | | 2005/06 | |
|  | Females % | Males % | Females % | Males % |
| --- | --- | --- | --- | --- |
| Denmark | 21 | 17 | 15 | 15 |
| England | 28 | 21 | 18 | 13 |
| France | 27 | 26 | 21 | 17 |
| Germany | 34 | 32 | 22 | 17 |
| Greenland | 67 | 57 | 48 | 37 |
| Ireland | 21 | 20 | 20 | 19 |
| Portugal | 26 | 18 | 12 | 9 |
| Russian Federation | 19 | 27 | 21 | 27 |
| Scotland | 23 | 16 | 23 | 14 |
| Sweden | 19 | 11 | 9 | 8 |
| USA | 12 | 18 | 9 | 7 |
| Wales | 27 | 16 | 23 | 12 |

SOURCE: Currie et al., (2008).

## 3.18 Proportion of pupils who drank alcohol in the last week, by gender and age, in England, 2007

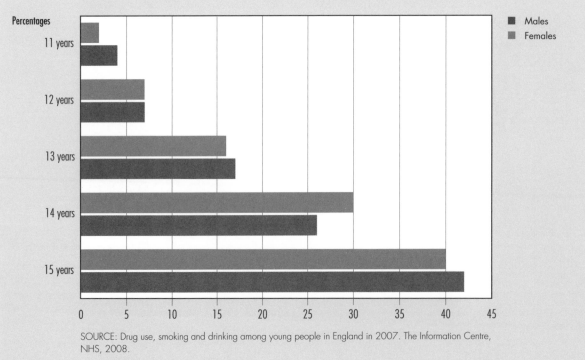

SOURCE: Drug use, smoking and drinking among young people in England in 2007. The Information Centre, NHS, 2008.

## 3.19 Mean units of alcohol consumed in last 7 days, among 11-15 year-olds, by gender, in England,1990-2007

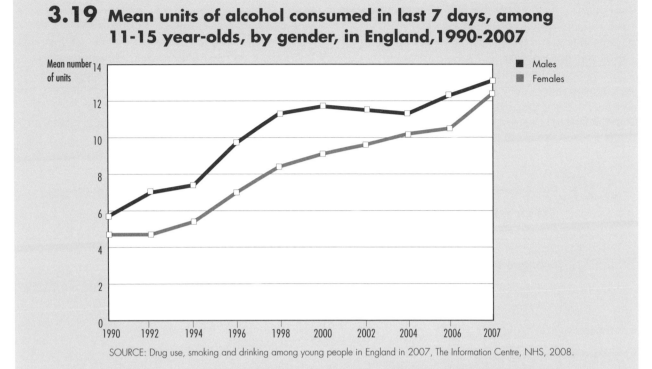

SOURCE: Drug use, smoking and drinking among young people in England in 2007, The Information Centre, NHS, 2008.

## 3.20 Average weekly alcohol consumption among 16-24 year-olds, by gender, in England, 2006

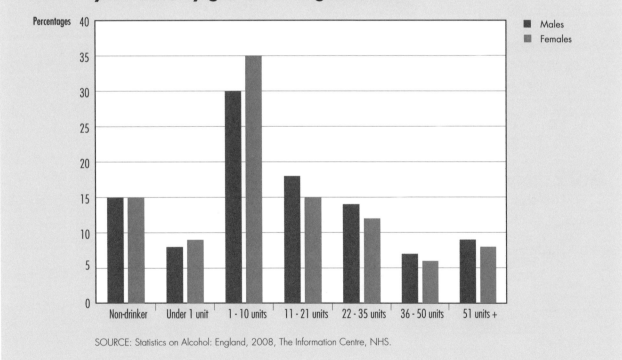

SOURCE: Statistics on Alcohol: England, 2008, The Information Centre, NHS.

The issue of alcohol misuse and especially binge drinking among young people has been an issue of concern for a number of years now. Consequently, we now turn to consider the data relating to alcohol consumption and adolescents. Figures in **Chart 3.18** indicate that alcohol intake increases dramatically with age, and that there is little differentiation by gender. In both 2005 and 2007, slightly higher proportions of girls at age 14 reported drinking alcohol in the last week, compared to boys (Information Centre 2006,

2008). This indicates that 14 years (year 9) may be an important age to specifically target girls for alcohol-related health promotion interventions.  Looking at 11-15 year-olds as a whole and considering the mean number of alcohol units drunk over a 7 day period, **Chart 3.19** provides evidence of a dramatic doubling in the amount of alcohol consumed by 11-15 year-olds since 1990. In addition, the 2007 data illustrates that one area where younger teenage girls are closing a gender gap is in the amount of alcohol units consumed.

Turning to late adolescence and early adulthood, **Chart 3.20** demonstrates that 30% of young men aged 16-24 regularly drink more than the recommended 21 units of alcohol a week and that 25% of young women exceed the recommended 14 units for women. International comparisons reveal the high prevalence of drinking to excess within the UK.

**Chart 3.21** highlights that early drunkenness at or before the age of 13 is relatively more frequent in northern European countries, such as Austria (26% of boys), compared to southern European countries such as Italy, (6% of boys). However, the chart also illustrates that among the countries of the UK included in the HBSC study, early drunkenness is among the highest reported for any country in the European Union. In the HBSC study, the ranking of the UK countries against all included countries for early drunkenness is as follows, England (4th), Wales (5th) and Scotland (8th), (Currie et al., 2008).

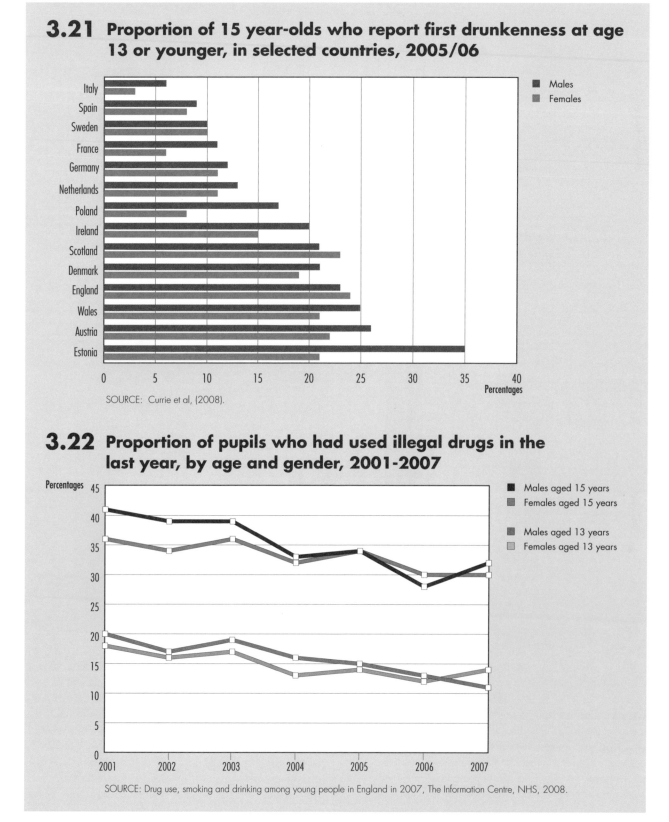

**3.21** **Proportion of 15 year-olds who report first drunkenness at age 13 or younger, in selected countries, 2005/06**

SOURCE: Currie et al, (2008).

**3.22** **Proportion of pupils who had used illegal drugs in the last year, by age and gender, 2001-2007**

SOURCE: Drug use, smoking and drinking among young people in England in 2007, The Information Centre, NHS, 2008.

There is a considerable amount of data relating to substance and illegal drug misuse among young people. However, not all findings are consistent as this is a challenging area to research and self-report studies have obvious potential limitations. The Office for National Statistics carries out one of the most reputable series of studies. **Chart 3.22** reports on the proportion of illegal drug use among the school population aged 13-15.

Overall, the percentage of the school-aged population who had used illegal substances in the last year has seen a slight downward trend since 2001. In a similar pattern to other risk behaviours, illegal drug use increases by age. In 2007, 11% of 13 year-old boys and 14% of girls had taken illegal drugs; among 15 year-olds, these figures increased to 32% of boys and 30% of girls. Since 2004, there has been a marked closing of any gender gap, so that among girls aged

### 3.23 Proportion of pupils aged 11-15 years who took illegal drugs, by type and class of drug, in 2007

Percentages

|  | 11 years | 12 years | 13 years | 14 years | 15 years |
|---|---|---|---|---|---|
| Class A |  |  |  |  |  |
| Cocaine | 0.3 | 0.4 | 1.1 | 2.5 | 4.3 |
| Crack | 0.3 | 0.7 | 0.6 | 1.9 | 1.3 |
| Ecstasy | 0.2 | 0.1 | 0.9 | 1.8 | 2.9 |
| **Any class A drugs** | **0.8** | **1.3** | **2.4** | **6.2** | **7.9** |
| **Any psychodelics** | **0.5** | **0.2** | **0.9** | **3.4** | **3.9** |
| **Any opiates** | **0.3** | **0.4** | **0.7** | **1.2** | **0.7** |
| Cannabis | 0.8 | 1.9 | 4.7 | 13.7 | 22.2 |
| Glue, gas, aerosols or solvents | 4.4 | 4.1 | 6.1 | 8.8 | 7.1 |
| **Any drug** (excl. volatile substances) | **1.8** | **4.1** | **7.5** | **19.2** | **28.7** |
| **Any drug** | **6.1** | **7.7** | **12.4** | **24.2** | **31.1** |

SOURCE: Drug use, smoking and drinking among young people in England, in 2007, The Information Centre, NHS, 2008.

### 3.24 Proportion of 15 year-olds who have ever used cannabis, in selected countries, 2008

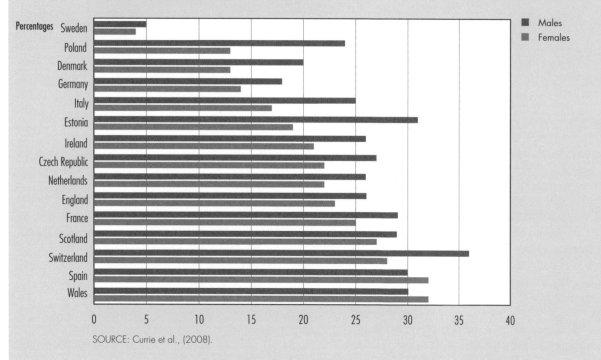

SOURCE: Currie et al., (2008).

15 substance misuse now effectively mirrors that of boys. In **Chart 3.23** the age distribution of forms of substance misuse can also be seen, showing that use of any drug increases dramatically for 14 and 15 year-olds. It is particularly noteworthy that the use of cannabis more than trebles between 13 and 14 years and then almost doubles again from 14 to 15 years. International comparisons in relation to cannabis use for 15 year-olds are presented in **Chart 3.24**. Although Switzerland has a very high rate of cannabis use, 15 year-olds in England, Scotland and Wales remain among the highest users. Since 2002, cannabis use has decreased in England, while it has increased slightly in Wales. It is also important to note that countries from the former Soviet Bloc such as Estonia, Czech Republic and Poland all have very high rates of cannabis use. It is unclear if this is an issue among young people who have migrated to the UK from these countries.

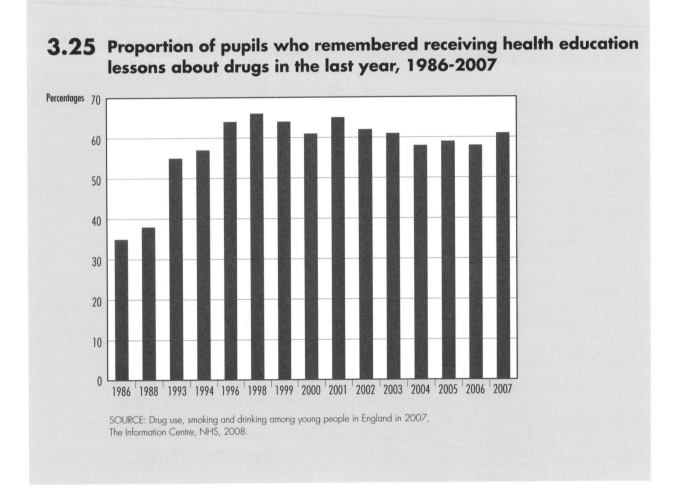

## 3.25 Proportion of pupils who remembered receiving health education lessons about drugs in the last year, 1986-2007

SOURCE: Drug use, smoking and drinking among young people in England in 2007, The Information Centre, NHS, 2008.

In view of the importance of health promotion within the school curriculum, **Charts 3.25** and **3.26** consider young people's own perspectives on substance misuse education within schools. **Chart 3.25** illustrates that although there have been minor fluctuations since 1993, the proportion of pupils who remembered receiving drug-related health education lessons has remained relatively stable at about 60%. **Chart 3.26** presents findings relating to pupils' perceptions about the effectiveness of health education. The majority of pupils viewed the lessons positively in terms of increasing knowledge about risk and sources of help and advice. Interestingly, those who had taken drugs more recently were less likely than other pupils to feel that the lessons had helped them to avoid future drug taking or given them strategies for managing high risk situations.

**Chart 3.27** provides an overview of the sources of information and support that young people report using for emotional and physical health issues. It is perhaps not surprising that among 12-14 year-olds peers feature strongly as sources of information and support. However, perhaps many adults and particularly parents might be surprised to learn that, with the exception of sex and relationships, many young people turn first to family for advice and information about a range of health-related and emotional issues. This finding illustrates the importance of support for parents in communicating with their teenage children.

## 3.26 How pupils felt lessons on drugs had helped them, by whether they had ever taken drugs, 2007

| | When last took drugs | | | |
|---|---|---|---|---|
| | In the last month | Taken drugs not in the last month | Never taken drugs | Total |
| | *Percentage who agreed with each statement* | | | |
| They helped me think about the risk of taking drugs | 87 | 95 | 97 | 95 |
| They helped me find out more about drug use | 85 | 91 | 90 | 90 |
| They helped me realise that taking some drugs is against the law | 77 | 82 | 85 | 84 |
| They helped me to avoid drugs | 50 | 75 | 84 | 80 |
| They helped me think about what I would do if someone offered me drugs | 65 | 72 | 79 | 77 |
| They helped me find out where to go to get information or help about drugs | 74 | 74 | 71 | 72 |
| They helped me understand why people take drugs | 72 | 70 | 66 | 68 |
| They helped me see that not as many young people take drugs as I thought | 39 | 39 | 38 | 39 |

SOURCE: Drug use, smoking and drinking among young people in England in 2007, The Information Centre, NHS, 2008.

## 3.27 Where do 12-15 year-olds go first for help or information about emotional and physical health issues?

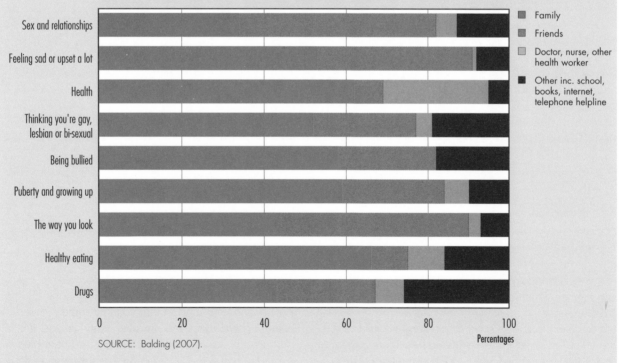

SOURCE: Balding (2007).

Turning back full circle to the start of this chapter, primary health care services also feature for 12-15 year-olds as a first source of advice and help. While many young people see doctors, nurses and health workers as a source of support for health issues, PHC professionals also feature as a potential first source of advice for a range of other issues relating to health behaviours, such as drug use and healthy eating. Which groups and ages of young people might find health workers helpful in such instances is currently unclear. However, these findings once again highlight the importance of primary health care services prioritising young people's health.

# References

Balding J (2007) *Young People into 2007.* Schools Health Education Unit. Exeter.

Brooks F and Magnusson J (2006). *Taking part counts: Adolescents' experiences of the transition from inactivity to active participation in school-based physical education.* Health Education Research: Special Edition Childhood Obesity 21(6) 872-883.

Craig R and Mindell J (eds) (2008) *Health Survey for England 2006, Vol 2, Obesity and Other Risk Factors in Children.* The Information Centre, Lifestyle Statistics. London.

Churchill R et al. (2000) *Do the attitudes and beliefs of young teenagers towards general practice influence actual consultation behaviour?* British Journal of General Practice, 50 953-97.

Coleman J and Schofield J (2007) *Key Data on Adolescence 2007, 6th Edition.* Trust For The Study Of Adolescence. Brighton.

Currie C and Roberts C et al. (2004) *Young People's Health in Context: Health Behaviour in school-aged children (HBSC) study: international report from the 2001/2002 survey.* Copenhagen, The World Health Organisation. Geneva.

Currie C et al. (2008) *Health behaviour in school-aged children (HBSC) study. International report from the 2005/06 study. World Health Organisation.* Centre for Adolescent Health Research Unit, University of Edinburgh.

Department of Health (2004a) *Choosing health.* Department of Health, London.

Department of Health (2004b) *National service framework for children, young people and maternity services.* Department of Health, London.

DfES (2003) *Every Child Matters.* The Stationery Office, London.

Donaldson L (2008) *On the State of Public Health: Annual Report of the Chief Medical Officer, 2007.* Office for National Statistics. The Stationery Office. London.

Hawkins J, Catalano R, Kosterman R, Abbott R and Hill K (1999). *Preventing adolescent health-risk behaviors by stengthening protection during childhood.* Archives of Pediatrics and Adolescent Medicine 133 (March), 227-234.

Morgan A, Malam S, Muir J and Barker R (2006) *Health and social inequalities in English adolescents: exploring the importance of school, family and neighbourhood. Findings from the WHO Health Behaviour in school-aged children study.* NICE. London.

The NHS Information Centre (2006) *Smoking, Drinking and Drug Use among young people in England in 2005.* The Information Centre. London.

The NHS Information Centre (2008) *Statistics on Obesity, Physical Activity and Diet: England.* January. The Information Centre. London.

The NHS Information Centre (2008) *Statistics on Smoking, England 2008.* The Information Centre. London.

The NHS Information Centre (2008) *Smoking, Drinking and Drug Use among young people in England in 2007.* The Information Centre. London.

The NHS Information Centre (2008) *Statistics on Alcohol: England 2008.* May. The Information Centre. London.

# CHAPTER

## Secondary Care, Long-term Conditions and Disability

**4**

KEY MESSAGES

### Gender differences in death rates

There is a marked gender difference in mortality rates, with more than double the number of males than females dying in adolescence and early adulthood (Chart 4.1)

### Increased emergency admissions

While the number of young people admitted to hospital as emergency admissions has steadily increased since the mid-1990s, between 2002 and 2007, emergency admissions among the 16-19 age group increased by a dramatic 32% (Chart 4.4)

### Rising level of long-term conditions

Hospital admissions among 10-19 year-olds for diabetes, asthma and epilepsy – the three most common long-term conditions affecting young people – increased by just over 13% over the past 5 years, from 149,400 in 2002/03 to 169,200 in 2006/07 (Chart 4.6)

### An absence of good data

Adolescence as a category is invisible in the way that much of the information relating to the secondary care system is presented. Data that includes young people is often collated for much broader age groups and there is a paucity of data in a number of key areas.

## Secondary Care, Long-term Conditions and Disability

While is it true that young people tend to be healthier than other age groups, this fact can result in adolescent health needs due to illness or long-term conditions being overlooked both within health policy and service planning, and even data collection. However, as will be explored in this chapter, high numbers of young people are affected by poor health, including long-term conditions and disability. In terms of self-rated health alone, the most recent WHO Health Behaviour in School Aged Children Study (Currie et al., 2008) reported that among 15 year-olds from England, Scotland and Wales 32-34% girls and 18%-20% of boys rated their health as fair or poor, compared to only 13% of Spanish 15 year-old girls and 6% of boys. Poor health during adolescence can have long-term effects on life chances, by preventing the attainment of educational goals and restricting psychological development (Currie et al., 2008). The recent CMO's report (Donaldson, 2008), recommended that in the light of the significant effects of poor health during the teenage years *"new approaches are needed to make health programmes and health services more teen-centred."* (p15).

A key element of understanding young people's health status and consequently their health needs is a robust evidence base. However, adolescence represents something of an invisible category in the way that much data relating to the secondary care system is interpreted and presented. Data that include young people are often collated as 0-19 or even 14-59 years. In a number of key areas, such as disability, and eating disorders, there is a paucity of national data and existing data sets that urgently require updating.

In this chapter, we firstly consider mortality among young people. Chart 4.1 illustrates that, aside from infant mortality, death rates among young people are highest in late adolescence (15-19 years) and even higher in early adulthood (20-24). The change with age is primarily due to deaths caused by injury and self-poisoning, as well as traffic accidents. The figures in **Chart 4.1** demonstrate a marked gender difference, with more than double the number of males than females dying in these age groups. However, since 2004, there has been a slight decrease in the number of deaths among young people across both sexes.

If we turn to the impact of disease and deaths from life-limiting conditions, **Chart 4.2** describes the range of conditions likely to have required palliative care among young people. Deaths in adolescence from disease and ill health are less common than for other age groups. However, as the recent Chief Medical Officer's Report (Donaldson, 2008) noted, mortality from such causes still represents a significant number

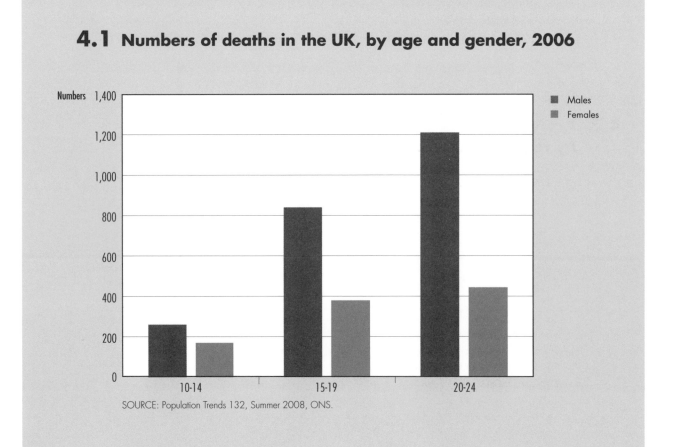

**4.1** **Numbers of deaths in the UK, by age and gender, 2006**

SOURCE: Population Trends 132, Summer 2008, ONS.

of teenage deaths per year. If the numbers of deaths from injury, poisoning, mental and behavioural disorders and other external causes reported in **Chart 4.2** are excluded, then deaths from diseases and conditions requiring palliative care between 2001 and 2005 accounted for 4,083 adolescent deaths (10-19 years). Deaths from malignant neoplasms or cancers and diseases of the nervous system such as muscular dystrophies, multiple sclerosis and auto-immune diseases accounted for the main causes of disease-

related mortality among young people (2,309 deaths). In addition, the late effects of congenital abnormalities accounted for nearly 500 deaths over the five-year period. **Chart 4.3** provides an overview of regional differences in the extent of mortality of young people within England. These statistics highlight regional variations in levels of need for palliative care services for young people, including a high level of need within London.

## 4.2 Deaths from causes likely to require palliative care for ages 10-14, 15-19 and 20-24, in England, 2001-2005

Numbers

|  | 10-14 | 15-19 | 20-24 |
|---|---|---|---|
| Congenital malformations, deformations and chromosomal abnormalities | 206 | 274 | 270 |
| Diseases of the nervous system | 410 | 605 | 483 |
| Neoplasms | 543 | 749 | 921 |
| Certain conditions originating in the perinatal period | 4 | 11 | 4 |
| Diseases of the circulatory system | 131 | 336 | 427 |
| Endocrine, nutritional and metabolic diseases | 114 | 166 | 215 |
| Diseases of the blood and blood-forming organs and certain disorders involving the immune mechanism | 70 | 78 | 89 |
| Diseases of the genitourinary system | 37 | 62 | 88 |
| Diseases of the digestive system | 20 | 41 | 102 |
| Diseases of the musculoskeletal system and connective tissue | 55 | 88 | 45 |
| Diseases of the respiratory system | 12 | 31 | 35 |
| Injury, poisoning and certain other consequences of external causes | 24 | 45 | 44 |
| Certain infectious and parasitic diseases | 21 | 19 | 28 |
| Mental and behavioural disorders | 5 | 3 | 5 |
| External causes of morbidity and mortality | 3 | 8 | 19 |

SOURCE: Cochrane H et al. (2007) Palliative Care Statistics for Children and Young Adults. Health and Care Partnerships Analysis, Dept. of Health.

## 4.3 Average number of deaths per year from all causes, by region, 2002-2005

Numbers

|  | 0-19 years | 20-29 years |
|---|---|---|
| East Midlands | 298 | 295 |
| East of England | 341 | 353 |
| London | 531 | 556 |
| North East | 176 | 209 |
| North West | 503 | 498 |
| South Central | 227 | 244 |
| South Coastal | 243 | 253 |
| South West | 276 | 306 |
| West Midlands | 391 | 362 |
| Yorkshire & the Humber | 404 | 402 |
| All Strategic Health Authorities | 3,388 | 3,476 |
| **England total** | **3,641** | **3,750** |

SOURCE: Cochrane H et al. (2007) Palliative Care Statistics for Children and Young Adults. Health and Care Partnerships Analysis, Dept. of Health.

## 4.4 Emergency admission to hospital by age group, in England, 1996/97-2006/07

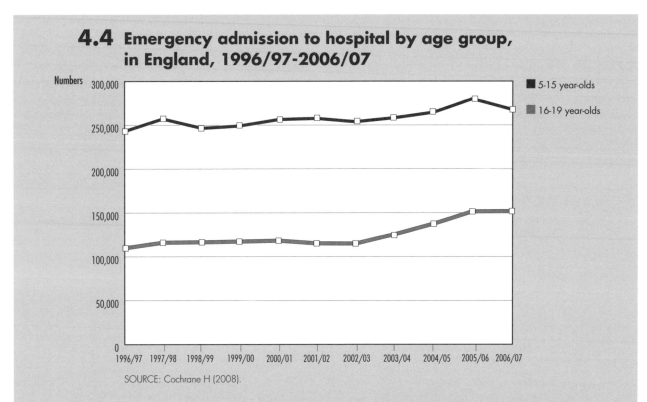

SOURCE: Cochrane H (2008).

## 4.5 Number of hospital admissions of under-18s for alcohol-related diseases, in England, 1997-2006

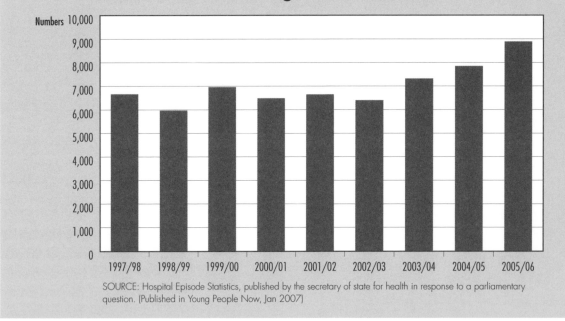

SOURCE: Hospital Episode Statistics, published by the secretary of state for health in response to a parliamentary question. (Published in Young People Now, Jan 2007)

Turning to young people's use of secondary care services, **Chart 4.4** illustrates an increasing pattern of emergency admissions to hospital for young people since 1996/97. The majority of emergency hospital admissions are for younger children aged 0-4, although approximately 18% are for young people aged 16-19 years. Between 2003 and 2007, emergency admissions for 5-15 year-olds saw a 5% increase; among the 16-19 age group admissions increased by a dramatic 32%. In all age groups, this rise in admissions was mainly from an increased number occurring via A&E departments (Cochrane, 2008).

**Charts 4.5** and **4.6** show in more detail the rates of hospital admissions for specific conditions that have a significant impact on adolescent health. The previous chapter highlighted the high levels of alcohol consumption and binge drinking among young people. **Chart 4.5** demonstrates an alarming rise in hospital admissions for young people since 1997. The admissions statistics for alcohol-related diseases consist of the three most common types of alcohol-related diseases: alcoholic liver disease, alcohol poisoning, and mental and behavioural disorders. The majority of young people are admitted to hospital with alcohol poisoning, which tends to occur from binge drinking. Young people are especially vulnerable to the poisoning effects of alcohol, due to body mass and metabolic handling of alcohol and relative inexperience in assessing alcohol-related risk (Miller et al., 2001).

Young people are also at risk of hospital admissions as a result of having a long-term or chronic condition. **Chart 4.6** presents statistics on hospital admissions for three specific conditions that have a high prevalence rate among young people, namely,

diabetes, asthma and epilepsy. The chart shows a concerning rise in hospital admissions among young people with these long-term conditions. In 2002/03, there were 149,373 admissions for 10-19 year-olds across the three conditions, just 5 years later in 2006/07 this had increased to 169,239 admissions, or by just over 13%. The rise was highest for asthma admissions which increased by 11,291 (19%) over the same period.

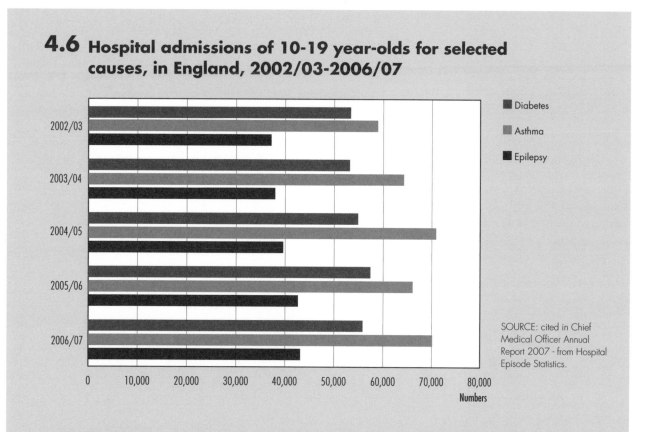

## 4.6 Hospital admissions of 10-19 year-olds for selected causes, in England, 2002/03-2006/07

SOURCE: cited in Chief Medical Officer Annual Report 2007 - from Hospital Episode Statistics.

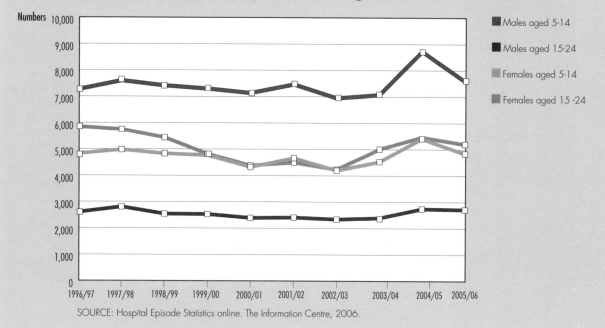

## 4.7 Finished consultant episodes with a primary diagnosis of asthma, by age and gender, in England, 1996/97-2005/06

SOURCE: Hospital Episode Statistics online. The Information Centre, 2006.

It is widely accepted that effective management of conditions such as asthma and diabetes can prevent hospital admissions. Consequently, these rates of hospital admissions give rise to questions about the standards of care for young people with long-term and chronic conditions.  A recent study of asthma in school-aged children in two UK cities found strong evidence that peaks in hospital admissions coincide with the end of the summer school holidays and the return to school (Julious et al., 2007). The reasons for this are not yet apparent, but the management of asthma within the school setting is likely to merit closer attention.

Although most asthma is managed within a PHC context, the rising number of hospital admissions suggests that the levels of consultant care episodes are also worthy of examination. **Charts 4.7** and **4.8** consider in more detail the usage of secondary care services by young people with asthma and allergies. The data presented is for finished consultant episodes. These are taken from hospital admissions statistics and refer to a period of care under one consultant, within one provider. **Chart 4.7** demonstrates that the numbers of young people for each age group under

consultant care for asthma, although fluctuating, has remained relatively stable across the last decade. There is, however, a marked disparity between older and younger males. Older males with asthma (15-24 years) demonstrate both the lowest rates of consultant care and the most stable rates of consultation, while boys aged 5-14 have the highest rates of consultant care.

In contrast, the numbers of young women under consultant care for both age groups track each other fairly consistently.  These statistics highlight the need for a more refined understanding of asthma management strategies adopted by young people and the character of support they receive for their asthma, across different ages and by gender. **Chart 4.8** shows that the numbers of young people under consultant care with a primary diagnosis of allergies is lower across all age groups than for asthma. However, there does appear to be an upward trend across all age groups, and particularly among the 15-24 age group, for both sexes. Moreover, as for asthma, consultant care for allergies is highest among younger boys aged 5-14.

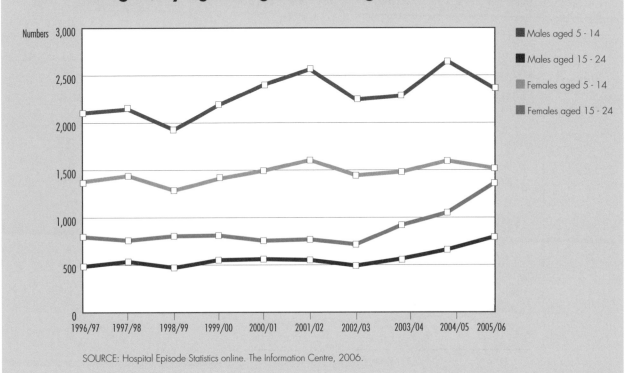

**4.8** **Finished consultant episodes with a primary diagnosis of allergies, by age and gender, in England, 1996/97-2005/06**

Legend:
- Males aged 5 - 14
- Males aged 15 - 24
- Females aged 5 - 14
- Females aged 15 - 24

SOURCE: Hospital Episode Statistics online. The Information Centre, 2006.

Among young people about 1,500 new cases of cancer are diagnosed each year in the UK, and more frequently occur in boys than girls (UK Childhood Cancer Research Group, 2004). **Chart 4.9** shows the prevalence of cancer and cancer registrations among adolescents. The commonest diagnoses are for leukemia, lymphoma and malignant brain tumors (Donaldson, 2008). Overall, there have been significant improvements in treatment for childhood cancer with the resulting improvement in survival. Consequently, there are many more adolescents and young adults living in the UK who have in the past been diagnosed with childhood cancer. Further research is needed to understand more fully the impact of cancer on their lives and their experiences.

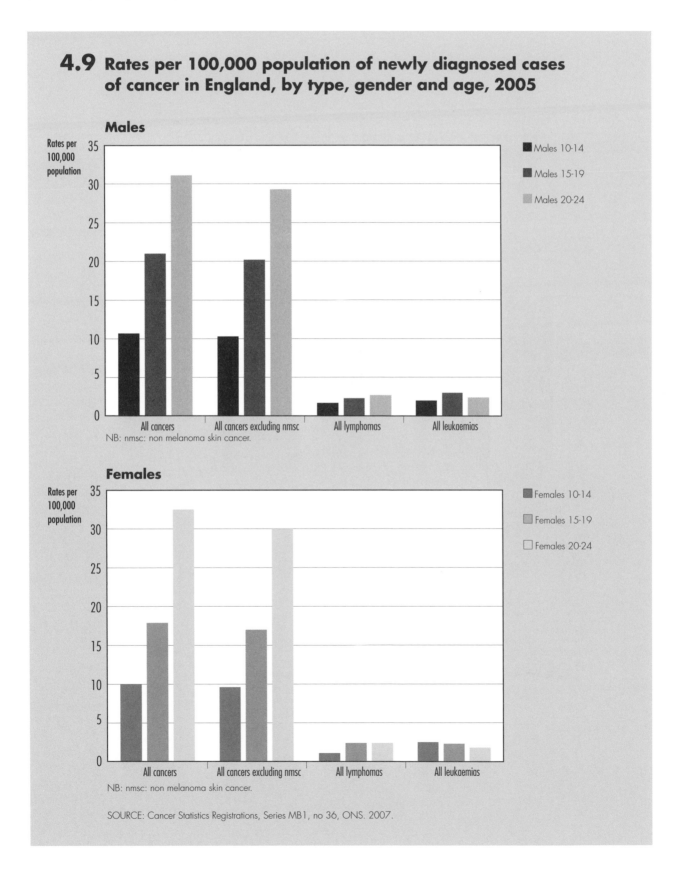

**4.9** **Rates per 100,000 population of newly diagnosed cases of cancer in England, by type, gender and age, 2005**

**Males**

NB: nmsc: non melanoma skin cancer.

**Females**

NB: nmsc: non melanoma skin cancer.

SOURCE: Cancer Statistics Registrations, Series MB1, no 36, ONS. 2007.

## 4.10 Incidence of anorexia nervosa and bulimia nervosa per 100,000 population in the UK, 2000

Incidence

| Age | Anorexia nervosa | | Bulimia nervosa | |
|---|---|---|---|---|
| | Female | Male | Female | Male |
| 10-19 | 35.8 | 3.4 | 34.6 | 2.3 |
| 20-39 | 28.6 | 1.0 | 10.5 | 0.5 |

SOURCE: Currin, Schmidt et al. (2005).

## 4.11 Age specific prevalence rates for population aged 5-19 years-old with a long-standing illness or disability, by gender, in Great Britain, 1990-2000

**Males**

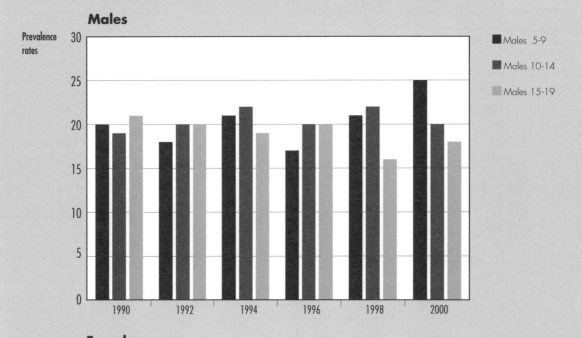

**Females**

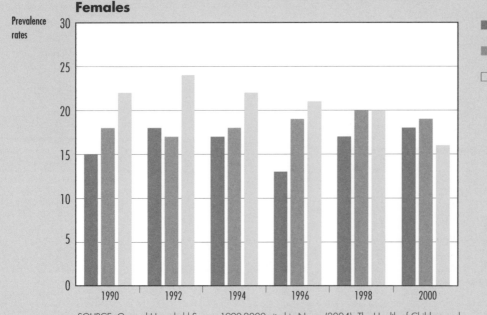

SOURCE: General Household Survey 1990-2000 cited in Nessa (2004) The Health of Children and Young People, Chapter 10, Disability. ONS.

Eating disorders consist of a number of syndromes that all have physical, psychological and social impacts. Anorexia nervosa and bulimia nervosa are the most commonly occurring forms of eating disorders, and are frequently chronic, long-term conditions with substantial physical, emotional and life-restricting consequences for the individual. Eating disorders usually develop in adolescence or young adulthood. Although estimates vary, **Chart 4.10** reports on the prevalence of anorexia nervosa and bulimia nervosa in 2000 as reported via primary health care practices (Currin et al., 2005).  The highest incidence rate for both conditions was found in young women aged 10-19. The rate for bulimia was slightly higher than for anorexia at 35.8 per 100,000 for young women aged 10-19 compared to 34.6 for anorexia. Currin et al. (2005) identified that the rates for bulimia represent a decline from peak incidence rates in the early 1990s. Services should target detection efforts at young women in the 10-19 age group who are most at risk for both conditions.

**Charts 4.11** to **4.13** look at the prevalence of disability and long-standing illness among young people. There is a paucity of up-to-date national data concerning disabled young people. This raises questions about the ability of services to undertake evidence-based strategic planning and service developments (Read, Spencer and Blackburn, 2007). Nessa (2004) employed two data sources, the General Household Survey 2000 (GHS) and the Family Fund

Trust's register of applicants, to examine the prevalence of disability among young people in Great Britain. **Chart 4.11** shows the prevalence of mild disability (defined as long-standing illness or disability) by age and gender, of which the most common condition is asthma, followed by autism and behavioural disorders. Young people aged 5-19 have higher rates of mild disability, when compared to the 0-4 age group. This is not surprising given that some conditions are more likely to emerge in later childhood while diagnoses of other conditions such as autism, may take a number of years.

The data reported in **Chart 4.11** reveals that the prevalence rates of mild disability across the decade remained relatively stable at about 20%, particularly in the 10-14 and 15-19 age groups. However in 1998, and in 2000, the year for which most recent data is available, there appears to have been a rise in the reported prevalence of mild disability among 5-9 year olds. An increased level of diagnosis of behavioural difficulties and conduct disorders could account for such a rise in rates among younger boys, as it is also known that boys are more likely than girls to suffer from behavioural disorders. Among girls in the 5-14 age groups, about 17% of the population report a mild disability or long standing illness. In the 15-19 age group, there appears to be a gradual decrease in prevalence. More recent national data is urgently required in order to determine longer-term trends among adolescents.

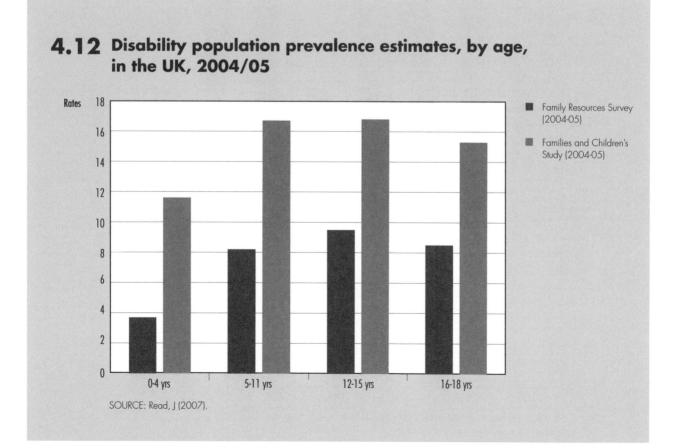

**4.12 Disability population prevalence estimates, by age, in the UK, 2004/05**

Legend:
- ■ Family Resources Survey (2004-05)
- ■ Families and Children's Study (2004-05)

SOURCE: Read, J (2007).

**Chart 4.12** presents findings from an ESRC-funded study (Read et al., 2007) that set out to undertake a detailed analysis of data from the Family Resources Survey and the Families and Children's study (2004-05) pertaining to disability among children. This study highlighted the complexity in accurately defining and determining prevalence rates for disability. The Families and Children's study identifies consistently higher rates of young people having one or more substantial difficulties with daily activities. However, both studies show that DDA–defined disability is lowest in the under 5s, thereby illustrating the significance for young people of disability acquired in middle childhood and adolescence.

The prevalence of severe disability is dispportionately reflected is some communities, particularly BME communities. **Chart 4.13** reveals that, in 2000, the BME communities with the highest prevalence rates of disability among young people aged 0-16 were the Pakistani and Black-African communities. The White and Chinese communities have the lowest prevalence of severe disabilities. These figures demonstrate the importance of developing culturally relevant and appropriate service provision for young people from Black African and Caribbean communities, and those from communities with a cultural heritage from the Indian Subcontinent.

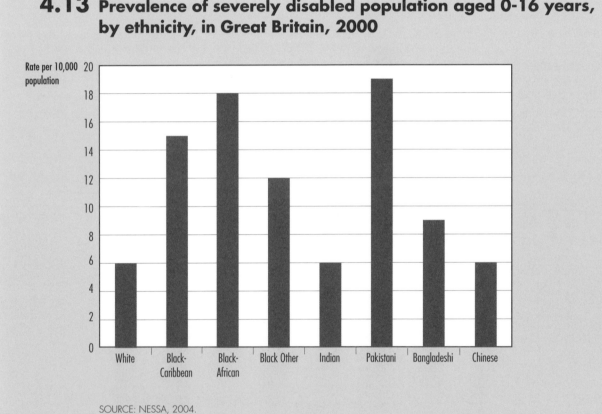

**4.13 Prevalence of severely disabled population aged 0-16 years, by ethnicity, in Great Britain, 2000**

SOURCE: NESSA, 2004.

# References

Cochrane H et al. (2007) *Palliative Care Statistics for Children and Young Adults Health Care.* Health Care Partnership Analysis. Department of Health. London.

Cochrane H (2008) *Trends in Children and Young Peoples' Care - Emergency Admission Statistics 1996/97-2006/07, England.* Chief Nursing Officers' Directorate, Department of Health. London.

Currie C et al. (2008) *Health behaviour in school-aged children* (HBSC) study. International report from the 2005/06 study. World Health Organisation. Centre for Adolescent Health Research Unit, University of Edinburgh.

Currin L, Schmidt U, Treasure J and Hershel J (2005) Time trends in eating disorder incidence. *British Journal of Psychiatry.* 186. 132-135.

Donaldson L (2008) *On the State of Public Health: Annual Report of the Chief Medical Officer, 2007.* July. ONS. London.

Julious S, Osman L and Jlwa M (2007) Increases in asthma hospital admissions associated with the end of summer vacation for school age children with asthma in two cities from England and Scotland. *Public Health.* Vol 121, Issue 6. 482-484.

Miller E, Kilmer J, Kim E, Weingardt K and Marlatt G (2001) Alcohol skills training for college students, in Monti P, Colby S and O'Leary T (eds) *Adolescents, Alcohol and Substance Abuse.* Guilford Press. New York. 183-215.

National Institute of Clinical Excellence (2004) *Eating Disorders: Core interventions in the treatment and management of anorexia nervosa, bulimia nervosa, and related eating disorders. National Clinical Practice Guideline Number CG9.* British Psychological Society and Royal College of Psychiatrists.

Nessa N (2004) Disability, in *The Health of Children and Young People.* Office for National Statistics. Stationery Office. London.

Office for National Statistics (2007) *Population Trends 132.* Stationery Office. London.

Office for National Statistics (2007) *Cancer Statistics Registrations.* Series MB1, No 36. London.

Read J, Spencer N and Blackburn C (2007) *Can we count them? Disabled children and their households.* Full Research Report. ESRC End of Award Report. RES-000-221725. ESRC. Swindon.

UK Childhood Cancer Research Group (2004) *National Registry of Childhood Tumors 2004.*

# CHAPTER 5

## Sexual Health

### Sexual experience

In England, over one quarter of boys and nearly one third of girls report having had sexual intercourse by the age of 15 (Chart 5.2)

### Falling teenage conceptions

Conception rates have fallen to their lowest levels and, in 2006, were at 40.4 per 1,000 young women aged 15-17 (Chart 5.4)

### Rising abortion rates

Rates of legal abortions among young women are increasing. In 2006, 49% of all conceptions among those under the age of 18 resulted in an abortion (Chart 5.12)

### Sexually transmitted infections

Sexually transmitted infections are still a worry. New diagnoses of chlamydia among those under 20 are continuing to rise, with 22,000 new cases being reported among young women in this age group in 2007 (Chart 5.19)

## Sexual Health

The sexual health of young people is a matter of intense public interest and concern. In recent years there has been a continuing focus on conception rates among young women in Britain. There has been much public discussion about suitable contraceptive services for young people and many secondary schools are now offering some form of sexual health service, even if it is just advice, as part of their provision for pupils. There has also been an intense focus on Sex and Relationships education and, at the time of writing, the Government has announced plans to make Personal, Social and Health Education (PSHE) a statutory element of the national curriculum. PSHE would include Sex and Relationships education. In addition to all this, the Teenage Pregnancy Unit continues to support and underpin a national strategy aiming both to reduce conceptions and to ensure better support for young parents. As we will see, the strategy is undoubtedly having an effect as conceptions rates are falling, albeit rather more slowly than the Government would like.

As far as research on the sexual behaviour of young people is concerned, it is still the case that there are far too few empirical studies that have been carried out in the UK. There have been a few notable exceptions, and we will consider one or two of these here. First, a team in Scotland have carried out a detailed survey of a large sample of 14 year-olds in their country (Wight and Henderson, 2000; Henderson et al., 2002). This is an unusual study, the first of its kind in Britain, and it enables us to get a sense of the range of sexual behaviour amongst this age group. Figures in **Chart 5.1** show that 18% of boys and 15% of girls report having had full sexual intercourse, whilst between a third and a half of the sample have engaged in heavy petting. These authors also provide evidence on the frequency of intercourse, reporting that among those who are sexually active, a third of the sample have only had sex once, and a further 52% have only had one sexual partner. Whilst this research is a few years old now, this remains the only UK study with such a young age group.

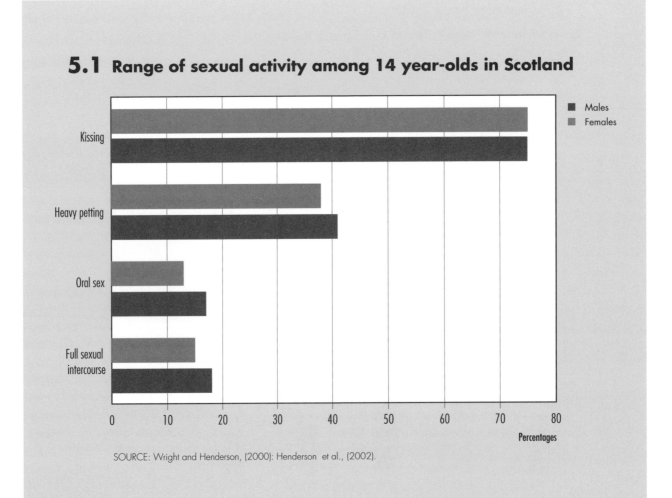

**5.1 Range of sexual activity among 14 year-olds in Scotland**

SOURCE: Wright and Henderson, (2000); Henderson et al., (2002).

The most up-to-date study of the sexual behaviour of young people is that which is carried out as part of the international Health Behaviour in School-Aged Children (Currie et al., 2008). The most recent stage was carried out in 2005/06, and results relating to the experience of sexual intercourse can be seen in **Chart 5.2**. Here it will be apparent that the UK countries fall broadly into the same range as other comparable European countries, with between 25% and 30% of young people aged 15 reporting having had sex by this age. It is of note that, in the UK countries, more girls than boys are reporting having had this experience. This is a big change from earlier studies where significantly more boys than girls reported being sexually active. It should also be noted that studies of sexual behaviour are notoriously difficult to carry out, especially with young people, and the reliability of the findings are always open to question. In the case of the results illustrated in **Chart 5.2**, it should be noted that this information is based on questions within a much larger survey of health behaviour, the survey being carried out in a classroom setting.

## 5.2 Experience of sexual intercourse as reported by 15-year olds, in Europe, 2005/06

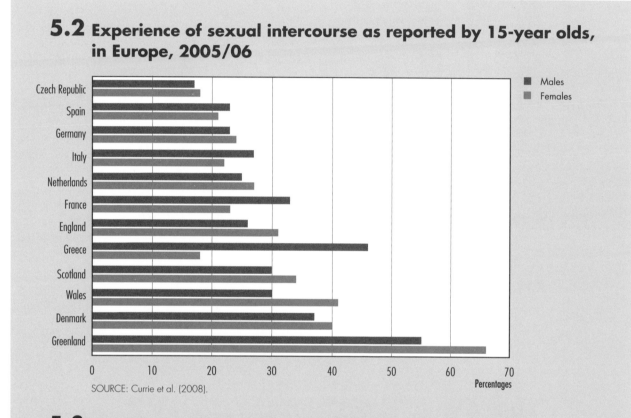

SOURCE: Currie et al. (2008).

## 5.3 Experience of sexual intercourse under 16 among all 16-18 year-olds, by ethnicity, 2005

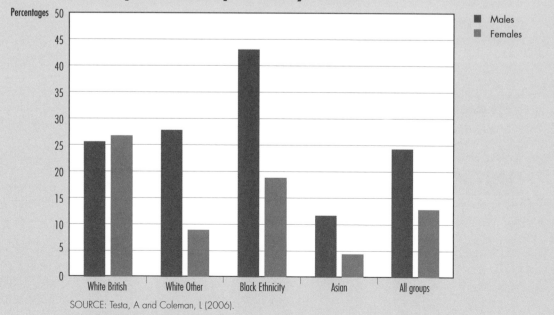

SOURCE: Testa, A and Coleman, L (2006).

## 5.4 Under 18 conception rates for England, 1998-2006

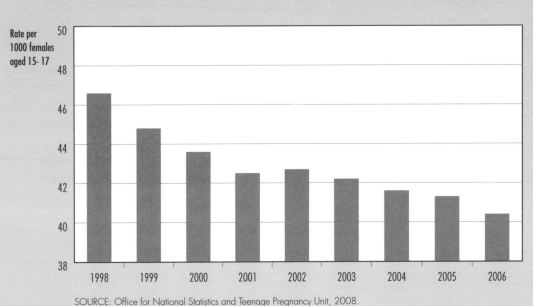

SOURCE: Office for National Statistics and Teenage Pregnancy Unit, 2008.

## 5.5 Under 18 conceptions and abortions in England, 1998-2006

| Year | Under 18 conceptions | Under 18 conception rate* | Percent leading to abortion |
|------|----------------------|---------------------------|-----------------------------|
| 1998 | 41,089 | 46.6 | 42.4 |
| 1999 | 39,247 | 44.8 | 43.5 |
| 2000 | 38,699 | 43.6 | 44.8 |
| 2001 | 38,461 | 42.5 | 46.1 |
| 2002 | 39,350 | 42.7 | 45.8 |
| 2003 | 39,553 | 42.2 | 46.1 |
| 2004 | 39,593 | 41.6 | 46.0 |
| 2005 | 39,804 | 41.3 | 46.8 |
| 2006** | 39,003 | 40.4 | 48.9 |

\* per thousand females aged 15-17
\** provisional

SOURCE: Office for National Statistics and Teenage Pregnancy Unit, 2008.

Another important perspective on sexual behaviour is provided by a recent study (Testa and Coleman, 2006) looking at experiences of sexual intercourse among young people in Britain from different ethnic backgrounds. Some results from this study are illustrated in **Chart 5.3**, where it can be seen that those from a Black background have significantly higher levels of sexual activity under the age of 16, while those from an Asian background have the lowest levels of all. These findings have enabled us to understand more about the relationship between culture and sexual health, and it is essential that this information is incorporated into both policy and practice.

We turn now to the question of teenage conception rates. We have already mentioned the work of the Teenage Pregnancy Unit. Readers will know that over the past decade there has been much public anxiety about the high rate of teenage conceptions in the UK, and about the unfavourable position this country occupies in having higher rates than other European countries. Evidence presented in **Chart 5.4** shows that the conception rates for women under the age of 18 in England have fallen steadily since 1998. This is encouraging evidence and clearly vindicates the Government's investment in its Teenage Pregnancy Strategy. The actual numbers and the rates per 1,000 population, together with the percentage of conceptions leading to abortions, are given in **Chart 5.5**.

Two important points need to be made about these figures. In the first place, in 2004, the Office for National Statistics developed revised population estimates for the country as a whole, and this has made it difficult to compare current conception rates with those of previous years. Conception rates shown in **Chart 5.5** are derived from revised population estimates. Secondly there are, of course, very wide regional variations in conception rates. As can be seen in **Chart 5.6,** while the East and the South East have low rates, those in London and in the North East are the highest in England.

## 5.6 Under 18 conception rates by region in England, 2006

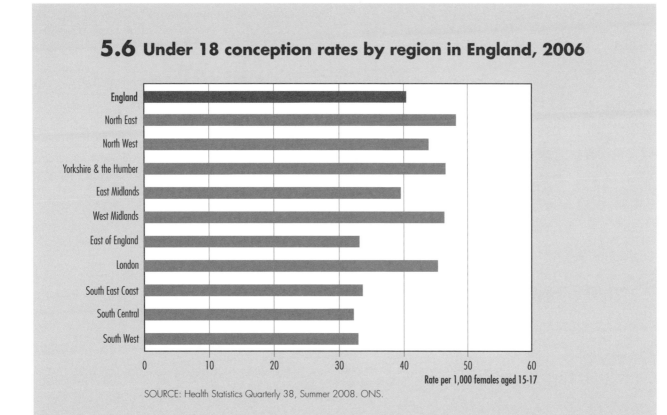

SOURCE: Health Statistics Quarterly 38, Summer 2008. ONS.

## 5.7 Conception rates for England, 13-15 year-olds, 1998-2006

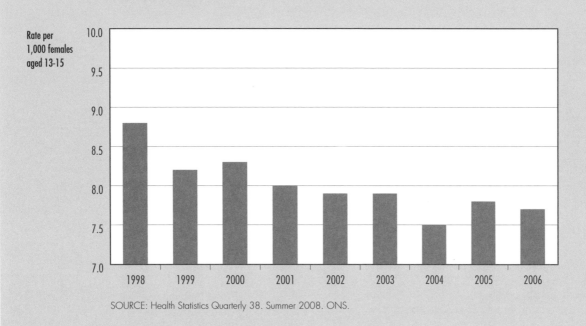

SOURCE: Health Statistics Quarterly 38. Summer 2008. ONS.

Turning now to those under the age of 16 in England, the most recent figures for this age group are illustrated in **Chart 5.7**. Here it can be seen that, again, there has been a steady fall in conception rates since 1998. The decline has been from 8.8 per 1,000 young women in 1998 to 7.7 per 1,000 young women in 2006. These figures are, once more, based on revised population estimates. We also show in **Chart 5.8** the actual numbers, the rates per 1,000 population and the percentage of conceptions leading to abortion. It is important to note that the rate of

decline in conception rates in England for both the under-18s and the under-16s has been remarkably similar. The decline since 1998 for the under-18s has been 12.9% and the decline for the under-16s has been 13.0%. Given the enormous challenge of reducing these rates, this is a significant achievement. Furthermore, the decline in the numbers of actual births has been even steeper as a result of increasing abortion rates, a topic we will return to below. The decline in births to the under-18 group has been of the order of 23% since 1998.

## 5.8  Under 16 conceptions and abortions in England, 1998-2006

| Year | Under 16 conceptions | Under 16 conception rate* | Percent leading to abortion |
|------|---------------------|---------------------------|------------------------------|
| 1998 | 7,855 | 8.8 | 52.9 |
| 1999 | 7,408 | 8.2 | 53.0 |
| 2000 | 7,620 | 8.3 | 54.5 |
| 2001 | 7,407 | 8.0 | 56.0 |
| 2002 | 7,395 | 7.9 | 55.7 |
| 2003 | 7,558 | 7.9 | 57.6 |
| 2004 | 7,181 | 7.5 | 57.6 |
| 2005 | 7,473 | 7.8 | 57.5 |
| 2006** | 7,296 | 7.7 | 60.3 |

\* per thousand females aged 13-15
\*\* provisional

SOURCE: Office for National Statistics and Teenage Pregnancy Unit, 2008.

## 5.9  Conception rates for Scotland, 13-15 year-olds, 1994-2006

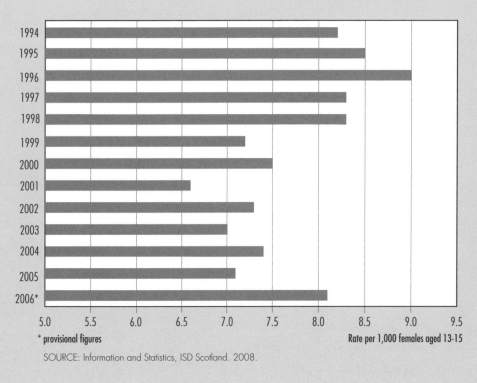

\* provisional figures

Rate per 1,000 females aged 13-15

SOURCE: Information and Statistics, ISD Scotland. 2008.

With regards to the situation in Scotland, it is difficult to compare rates across countries since the age groups used are not exactly the same. However, the most recent figures on conception rates in Scotland are illustrated in **Charts 5.9** and **5.10**. Although there was a gradual decline for both age groups from 1994 onwards, it appears that this decline has been halted over the last few years. Conceptions in the under-16 group were 8.1 per 1,000 young women in 2006, and those in the 16-19 year group were 58 per 1,000 women in the same year. There is no clear explanation for this trend, and it may be that the decline in rates will return in the coming years.

Conception rates are not available for Northern Ireland, but we can see the numbers of live births in the 15-19 year age group since 1990. As will be apparent from the figures in **Chart 5.11**, while rates have varied, there has been a gradual decline over the last decade or so, from 29.2 per 1,000 women in 1990 to 21.7% per 1,000 women in 2005.

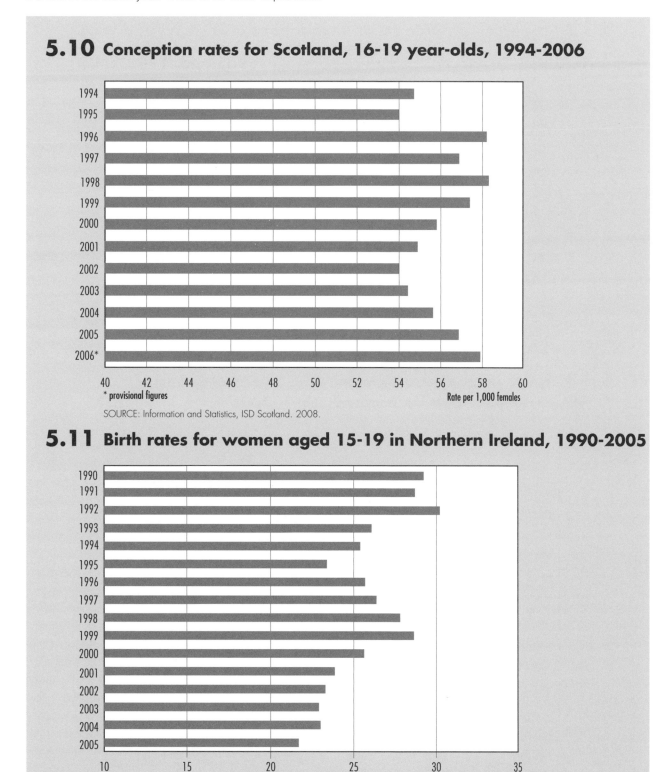

## 5.10 Conception rates for Scotland, 16-19 year-olds, 1994-2006

\* provisional figures

Rate per 1,000 females

SOURCE: Information and Statistics, ISD Scotland. 2008.

## 5.11 Birth rates for women aged 15-19 in Northern Ireland, 1990-2005

SOURCE: NISRA - Registrar General Annual Report 2005.

Rate per 1,000 females

As has been noted, although conception rates are of great importance, they only tell one side of the story. A further element of significance has to do with the proportion of conceptions that are terminated, in comparison with those that proceed to term and lead to a live birth. Readers will have noted that in **Charts 5.5** and **5.8**, we have shown the proportion of conceptions in the two age groups in England that lead to an abortion. These figures are combined in

**Chart 5.12** and show that a higher proportion of conceptions lead to abortion among the younger group than among the older group. This is as expected, but it still means that 40.2% of conceptions among those aged under 16 are leading to actual maternities. Some might question whether this is too high a figure but, as can be seen in **Chart 5.13**, there has been a gradual increase in the proportions of conceptions leading to an abortion among both age groups.

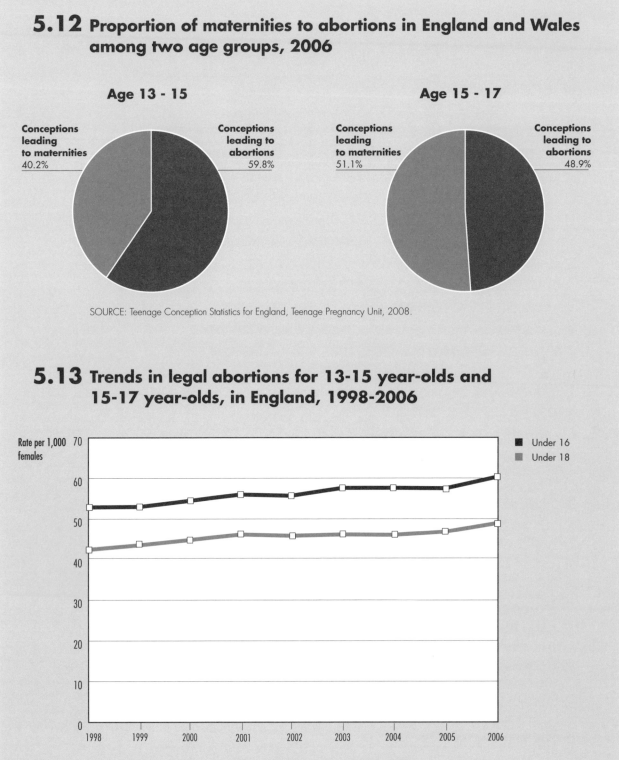

**5.12** **Proportion of maternities to abortions in England and Wales among two age groups, 2006**

Age 13 - 15

Conceptions leading to maternities 40.2%

Conceptions leading to abortions 59.8%

Age 15 - 17

Conceptions leading to maternities 51.1%

Conceptions leading to abortions 48.9%

SOURCE: Teenage Conception Statistics for England, Teenage Pregnancy Unit, 2008.

**5.13** **Trends in legal abortions for 13-15 year-olds and 15-17 year-olds, in England, 1998-2006**

Rate per 1,000 females

■ Under 16
■ Under 18

SOURCE: Teenage Conception Statistics for England, Teenage Pregnancy Unit, 2008.

## 5.14 Of all live births, percentage to mothers aged under 20 years in Europe, 2004

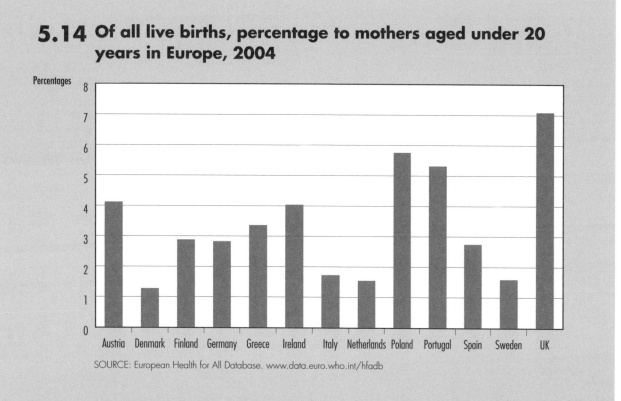

SOURCE: European Health for All Database. www.data.euro.who.int/hfadb

## 5.15 Of all live births, percentage to mothers aged under 20 years in the UK, 1977-2004

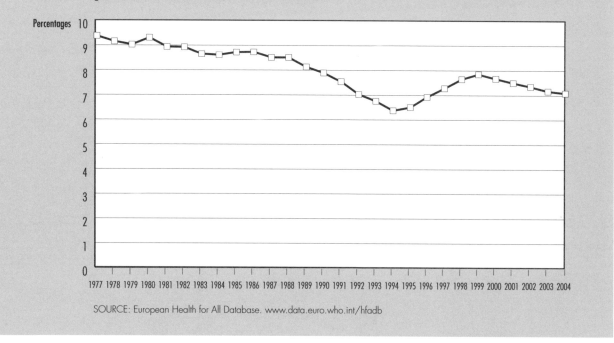

SOURCE: European Health for All Database. www.data.euro.who.int/hfadb

Again, as has already been noted, Britain compares poorly with other European countries in respect of teenage pregnancy. Statistics on conception rates are hard to find but figures shown in **Chart 5.14** illustrate that, where live births are concerned, the UK had significantly higher rates than other countries in 2004. However, there is some encouraging news, as figures illustrated in **Chart 5.15** show a gradual decline in the birth rate among this age group in the UK since 1977.

One important feature of the overall picture is that, as explained in the Social Exclusion Unit report "Teenage Pregnancy" (1999), birth rates in countries such as Germany, France and Italy were very similar to those in the UK in the 1970s. However, birth rates among young women aged 15-19 have fallen steadily since that time in most European countries, while rates in Britain have declined much more slowly during this period. It is not clear why this should be so but no doubt social and economic circumstances, as well as attitudes to sexual health and behaviour, all play their part.

We will now look at contraception. It can be seen from the data illustrated in **Chart 5.16** that, of those aged 15 attending community contraceptive clinics, 41% are using the contraceptive pill, whilst this figure rises to 49% in the 16-17 year age group, and to 53% in those aged between 18 and 19. As might be expected, the use of the condom decreases with age, from 60% in the under 15s to 27% in the 18-19 year-olds.

We have already mentioned the study by Testa and Coleman (2006), and this has useful information about contraceptive use and ethnicity. Figures shown in

**Chart 5.17** illustrate that ethnic background is a significant factor in this domain, with a clear difference being apparent between groups. Among Black Africans and Black Caribbeans, males are more likely not to use contraception at first intercourse, while among Asians, young women are more likely than their male counterparts not to use contraception at first intercourse. There are also very big overall differences between White young people and those from ethnic minority backgrounds. This has major implications for sex education policy, and it is to be hoped that more research of this nature will be undertaken in the near future.

## 5.16 Contraceptive use among women attending family planning clinics, by age, in England, 2006-07

Percentages

| Method | Under 15 | 15 | 16-17 | 18-19 | 20-24 | All ages |
|---|---|---|---|---|---|---|
| IU Devices | 0 | 0 | 0 | 1 | 3 | 6 |
| IU System | 0 | 0 | 0 | 0 | 1 | 3 |
| Injectable contraceptive | 2 | 4 | 6 | 8 | 10 | 8 |
| Implant | 2 | 2 | 3 | 5 | 5 | 4 |
| Oral contraceptives | 30 | 41 | 49 | 53 | 55 | 46 |
| Male condom | 60 | 46 | 36 | 27 | 21 | 28 |
| Female condom | 0 | 0 | 0 | 0 | 0 | 0 |
| Contraceptive patch | 0 | 0 | 0 | 1 | 1 | 1 |
| Natural family planning | 0 | 0 | 0 | 0 | 0 | 0 |
| Sterilisation | 0 | 0 | 0 | 0 | 0 | 0 |
| Other methods | 5 | 5 | 5 | 4 | 3 | 4 |

SOURCE: NHS Contraceptive Services, England 2006-07. The Information Centre, NHS.

## 5.17 First ever sexual intercourse: not used contraception, by ethnicity, 2005

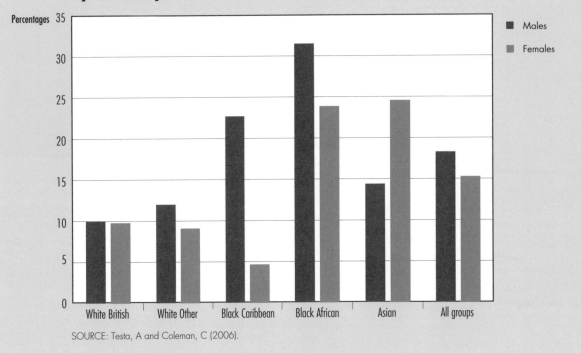

SOURCE: Testa, A and Coleman, C (2006).

One aspect of sexual health that has been receiving much greater attention in recent years is that of sexually transmitted infections. The main reason for this is a growing awareness of the steep increase over the past decade in the incidence of these infections, especially in young people. Figures in **Chart 5.18** give a picture of the range of problems which presented in GUM (genito-urinary medicine) clinics across the UK in 2007. As can be seen, both chlamydia and genital warts are infections presenting in significant numbers. It is hardly surprising that a high level of concern is being expressed by health professionals in relation to these infections. The nature of the time trend is illustrated in **Charts 5.19** and **5.20**. Where chlamydia is concerned there has been more than a 100% increase among young women aged 16-19 between 1998 and 2007. Furthermore, there is no sign that this increase is being halted. On the other hand, gonorrhoeal infection does seem to be declining since the high point of 2002 and 2003. There is little doubt that sexually transmitted infections among young people pose a significant challenge for health professionals.

## 5.18 New diagnoses of sexually transmitted infections, by gender and age, in the UK, 2007

Numbers

|  | Under 16 | | 16-19 | |
| --- | --- | --- | --- | --- |
|  | M | F | M | F |
| Infectious syphilis (primary and secondary) | 2 | 4 | 52 | 46 |
| Gonorrhoea (uncomplicated) | 40 | 206 | 1,742 | 2,120 |
| Genital chlamydia (uncomplicated) | 203 | 1,577 | 10,002 | 22,037 |
| Genital herpes (first attack) | 10 | 231 | 718 | 3,249 |
| Genital warts (first attack) | 104 | 763 | 5,311 | 12,856 |

SOURCE: Diagnoses of Selected STIs by Sex and Age Group, 2003-2007, UK, HPA.

## 5.19 New diagnoses of chlamydia infection presented at GUM clinics in the UK, among 16-19 year-olds, by gender, 1998-2007

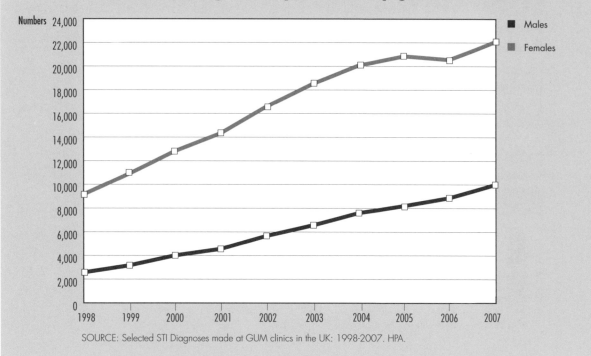

SOURCE: Selected STI Diagnoses made at GUM clinics in the UK: 1998-2007. HPA.

We will conclude this chapter with a brief look at some findings concerning knowledge of sexual health services and attitudes to sex education. Firstly, one striking finding reported in the Exeter survey (Balding, 2007) has to do with teenagers' awareness of services in their locality. It is worrying that, as can be seen from **Chart 5.21**, among Year 10 pupils in England, only 40% have knowledge of sexual health services available to them in their communities.

As far as attitudes to sex education are concerned, we will draw upon recent findings from the Health and Behaviour in School-Aged Children report (Currie et al.,

2008) already referred to earlier in this chapter. Findings illustrated in **Chart 5.22** show that, in Scotland, school is playing a key role in providing sex education, especially for boys. Friends are next on the list, followed by parents. However, as is shown in **Chart 5.23**, when it comes to indicating the person with whom it is easiest to talk about this subject, friends are almost the only group mentioned. This is a sobering thought, reflecting the fact that there is a long way to go before either parents or professional adults can easily engage with young people when discussing sexual health.

## 5.20 New diagnoses of gonorrhoea infection presented at GUM clinics in the UK, among 16-19 year-olds, by gender, 1998-2007

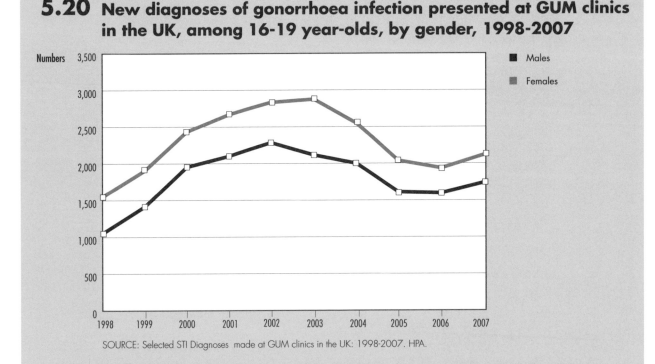

SOURCE: Selected STI Diagnoses made at GUM clinics in the UK: 1998-2007. HPA.

## 5.21 Answers to the question, "Is there a special birth control service for young people available locally?" among Year 10 pupils

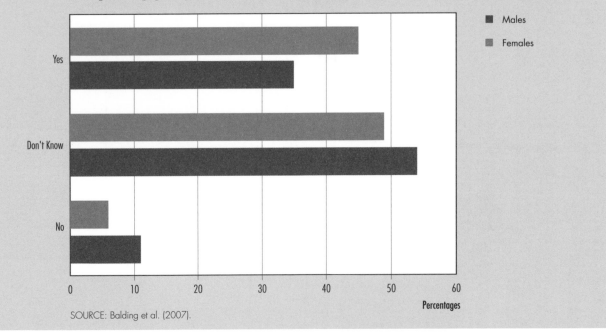

SOURCE: Balding et al. (2007).

**5.22** Main source of information on sexual matters among 11-15 year-olds in Scotland, by gender, 2006

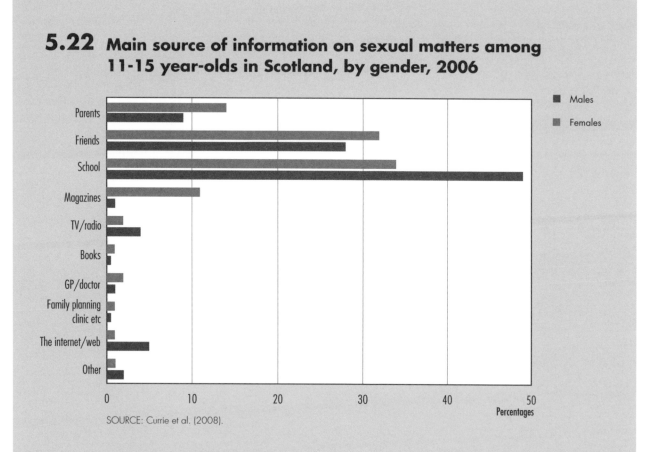

SOURCE: Currie et al. (2008).

**5.23** The person 11-15 year-olds find it is easiest to discuss personal and sexual health matters with, in Scotland, 2006

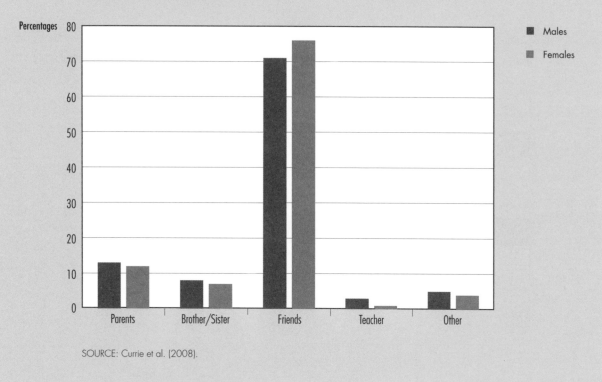

SOURCE: Currie et al. (2008).

# References

Balding J et al. (2007) *Young people into 2007*. Schools Health Education Unit.  Exeter University. Exeter.

Currie C et al. (2008) *Health behaviour in school-aged children* (HBSC) study. International report from the 2005/06 study. World Health Organisation. Centre for Adolescent Health Research Unit, University of Edinburgh.

Henderson M et al. (2002) Heterosexual risk behaviour among young people in Scotland. *Journal of Adolescence.* 25. 483-494.

Testa A and Coleman L (2006) *Sexual health knowledge, attitudes and behaviours among black and minority youth in London.* Trust for the Study of Adolescence and the Naz Project, London. Obtainable from www.tsa.uk.com

Wight D and Henderson M (2000) The extent of regretted sexual intercourse among teenagers in Scotland. *British Medical Journal.* 320. 1243-1244.

................. (1999) *Teenage pregnancy: a report by the Social Exclusion Unit*. The Stationery Office. London.

# CHAPTER

## Mental Health

**6**

### KEY MESSAGES

## Falling suicide rates

Suicide rates among young men in the UK have fallen steadily since 1994. In 2006, the rate among 15-24 year-olds was 10 per 100,000 population (Chart 6.1)

## Variations across the UK

There are substantial variations in suicide rates across the UK, with Northern Ireland and Scotland having significantly higher rates than England and Wales (Charts 6.2 - 6.4)

## Little change in psychiatric disorders

There has been little change over the past decade in the numbers of young people with a psychiatric disorder. For example, the proportion of boys so designated was 12.8% in 1999 and 13.1% in 2004 (Chart 6.12)

## Looked after children

45% of children and young people in the care of the local authority have a psychiatric disorder (Chart 6.15)

## More girls feel low

Girls are more likely than boys to report feeling low, with 45% of 15 year-old girls in England reporting feeling low during a one-week period. Young people in England are also more likely to report such feelings than their counterparts in the rest of the UK (Chart 6.18)

## Mental Health

Issues to do with the mental health of children and young people have been receiving considerable attention in the past few years. The whole country has been shocked by the spate of suicides among young people in South Wales during 2008, bringing to the fore uncomfortable questions about mental health and young people. More broadly, discussions about spending and resources have been contentious and there is a general perception that, in spite of increased Government funding, many services are being cut or are under threat. Research has questioned the performance of CAMHS services, and the evidence illustrates a situation which is hugely variable across different parts of the country. Waiting times vary widely, and the degree of integration of services with education, youth justice and social care is very much dependent on local structures and working practices.

There have also been questions raised over the use of drugs for children and young people, and reports originating from the National Institute for Clinical Excellence (NICE) have highlighted differing opinions about the use of treatments such as cognitive behaviour therapy and counselling. In addition to this, the last two or three years have seen a greatly increased focus on the whole question of well-being. The well-known UNICEF (2007) report, which showed British children in such a poor light, caused major political debate and partly as a result of this, schools in England and Wales have been asked to address issues to do with well-being.

Many have expressed concerns as to whether this is an appropriate area in which schools should intervene, and the debate has also raised questions about the links between mental health and mental illness. There is no doubt that this area of health has been much in the public mind. There is greater awareness today than there was in previous decades of the importance of this topic, and more attention is being paid to the vulnerability of certain populations such as those in care and those in custody.

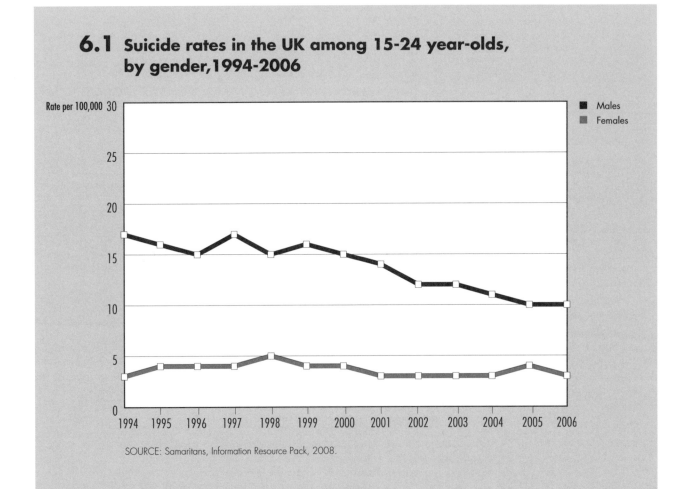

**6.1 Suicide rates in the UK among 15-24 year-olds, by gender, 1994-2006**

SOURCE: Samaritans, Information Resource Pack, 2008.

In this chapter we will start with a look at the statistics on suicide. It has been the hope and intention of governments for a number of years now to be able to reduce the suicide rates, especially the rates for young people. Looking at the rates for the UK as a whole shown in **Chart 6.1**, it can be seen that the rates for young men between the ages of 15 and 24 have come down gradually but surely since the mid-1990s. In 2006, the suicide rate for young men was 10 per 100,000 population, the lowest it has been for many years. This is a significant achievement, although it is difficult to be sure exactly which factors contribute to this trend. It is likely that economic conditions do play a major part and, as the coming recession starts to bite, we will need to keep a close eye on these figures. It should be noted that, as far as young women are concerned, there has been little change over the 12 year period, with rates remaining stable during this time.

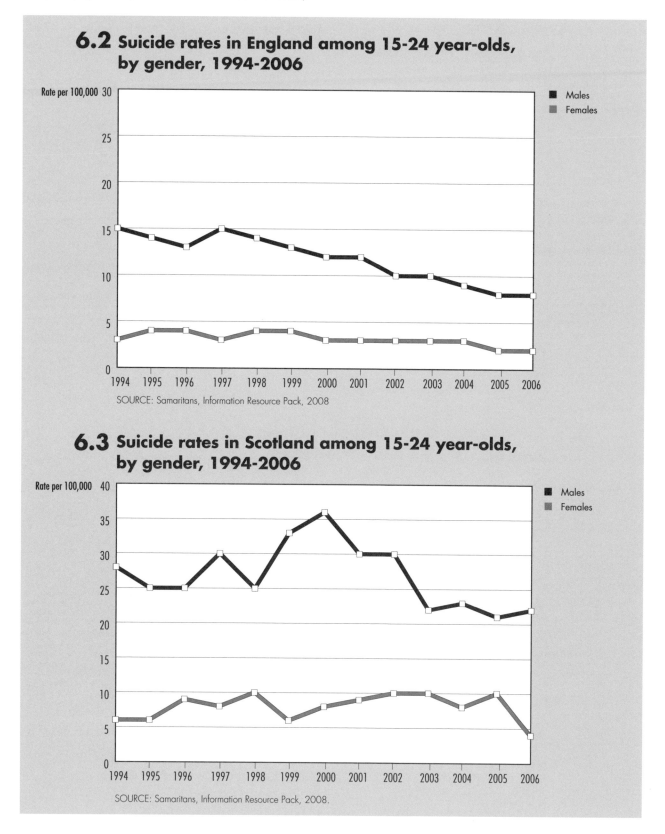

**6.2** Suicide rates in England among 15-24 year-olds, by gender, 1994-2006

Rate per 100,000

■ Males
■ Females

SOURCE: Samaritans, Information Resource Pack, 2008

**6.3** Suicide rates in Scotland among 15-24 year-olds, by gender, 1994-2006

Rate per 100,000

■ Males
■ Females

SOURCE: Samaritans, Information Resource Pack, 2008.

Turning to England, as can be seen in **Chart 6.2**, much the same is true here as it is of the UK in general, with rates declining slowly but steadily since 1994. The picture in Scotland, shown in **Chart 6.3**, is not so encouraging, with higher rates overall than in the UK for both young men and for young women. However, at least the very high levels for young men

seen in 1998 – 2001 are not being repeated. The situation in Northern Ireland is similar to that in Scotland, with higher rates than in the UK generally. Rates are illustrated in **Chart 6.4**. There has also been a very worrying and steep increase in rates for both males and females in the last two years. Suicide rates among young men and young women have more than

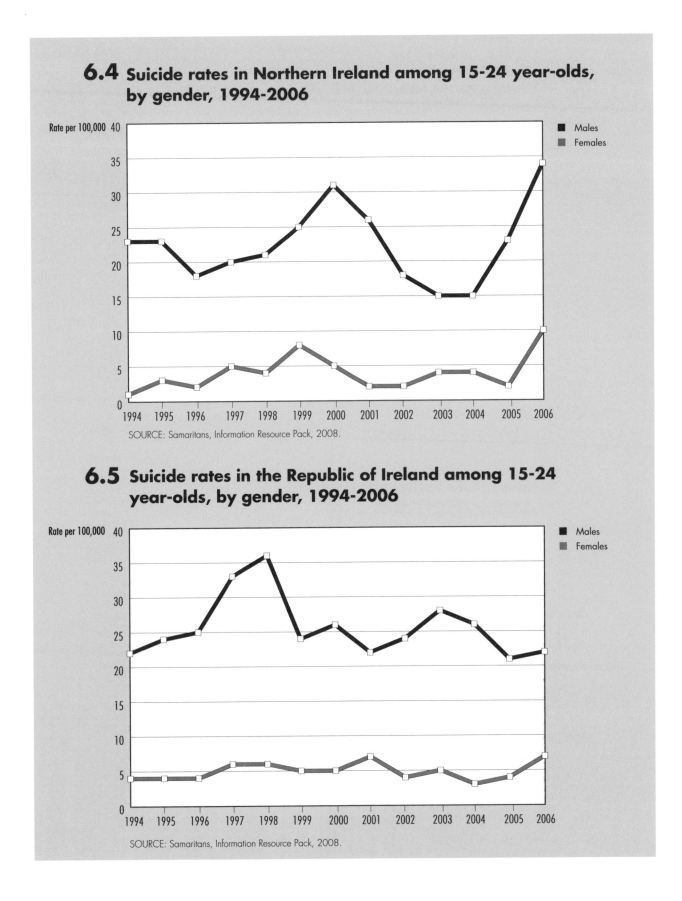

**6.4** **Suicide rates in Northern Ireland among 15-24 year-olds, by gender, 1994-2006**

SOURCE: Samaritans, Information Resource Pack, 2008.

**6.5** **Suicide rates in the Republic of Ireland among 15-24 year-olds, by gender, 1994-2006**

SOURCE: Samaritans, Information Resource Pack, 2008.

doubled in this period, with rates currently being 10 per 100,000 in young women and 34 per 100,000 for young men. These years have been a time of major political change in Northern Ireland although, as yet, there is no obvious explanation of the trend. This is clearly a situation that will need very careful monitoring.

We can also see the suicide rates in the Republic of Ireland illustrated in **Chart 6.5**. Here also, rates are higher than in the UK as a whole, but for young men there has been some decline in rates since the late 1990s.

## 6.6 Number of suicides and undetermined deaths in the UK, by age and gender, 1992-2006

Numbers

|  | 1992 | 1996 | 2000 | 2004 | 2006 |
|---|---|---|---|---|---|
| **Males** | | | | | |
| 0-14 | 19 | 22 | 21 | 13 | 12 |
| 15-24 | 690 | 560 | 550 | 412 | 431 |
| 25-34 | 1,061 | 1,153 | 1,033 | 773 | 756 |
| **Females** | | | | | |
| 0-14 | 10 | 9 | 11 | 8 | 10 |
| 15-24 | 151 | 149 | 142 | 130 | 112 |
| 25-34 | 284 | 269 | 257 | 202 | 192 |

SOURCE: Samaritans, Information Resource Pack, 2008.

## 6.7 Suicide rates among 15-19 year-olds, by gender, in EU countries, 2006

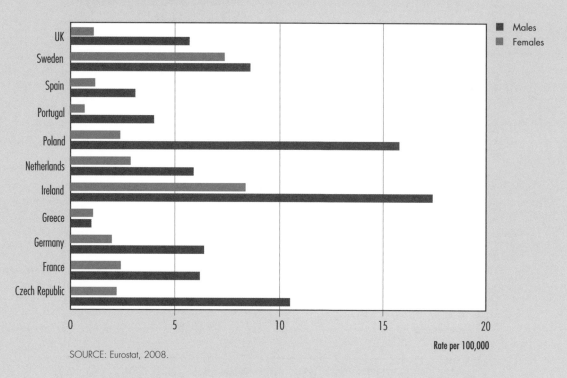

SOURCE: Eurostat, 2008.

It may be suggested that a discussion of rates is not a sufficiently powerful reflection of the real nature of the problem. While we can say that rates are falling in England and Wales, behind those statistics lie a catalogue of human misery and despair. A more graphic illustration of the problem is to consider the actual numbers and to recognise that, in 2006, a total of 431 young men between the ages of 15 and 24 lost their lives as a result of suicide. Comparisons of the actual figures for completed suicides in the UK for the years 1992, 1996, 2000, 2004 and 2006 are given in

**Chart 6.6**. It is encouraging to see that this also shows a significant drop in actual numbers, from 690 young men taking their lives in 1992 down to 431 young men doing so in the last year for which we have statistics.

Turning now to international comparisons, figures in **Chart 6.7** show that, while rates in the UK are above those in some European countries such as Spain, Portugal and Greece, there are many countries that have substantially higher rates than the UK. Readers

## 6.8 Self-harm thoughts and behaviour in last year, of 15-16 year-olds, by gender and country

Percentages

|  | Self-harm behaviour | | Self-harm thoughts | |
| --- | --- | --- | --- | --- |
|  | Males | Females | Males | Females |
| Australia | 1.7 | 11.7 | 8.6 | 21.7 |
| Belgium | 4.2 | 10.5 | 1.7 | 20.9 |
| England | 3.2 | 11.1 | 8.8 | 23.8 |
| Hungary | 1.7 | 6.2 | 17.5 | 33.2 |
| Ireland | 2.4 | 8.8 | 11.8 | 21.9 |
| Netherlands | 1.6 | 3.6 | 4.6 | 10.9 |
| Norway | 2.9 | 10.6 | 6.9 | 18.9 |

SOURCE: Madge, Hewitt et al. (2008).

## 6.9 Rates of deliberate self-harm in Oxford City, among 15-24 year-olds, by gender, 1994-2006

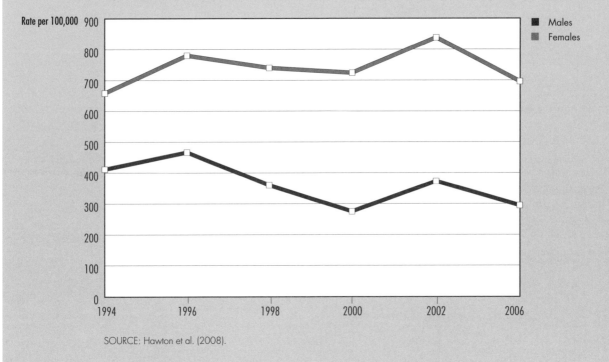

SOURCE: Hawton et al. (2008).

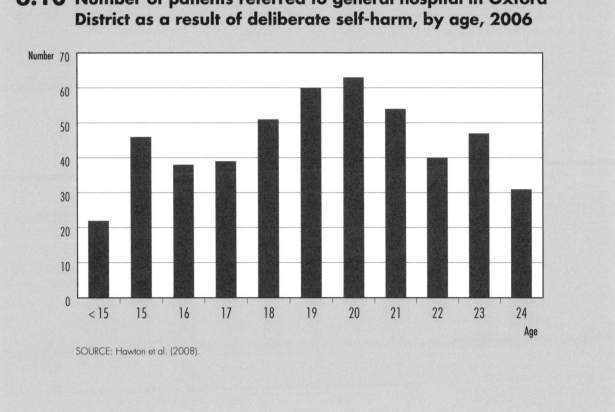

**6.10** **Number of patients referred to general hospital in Oxford District as a result of deliberate self-harm, by age, 2006**

SOURCE: Hawton et al. (2008).

may notice a lack of comparability between rates shown in the previous charts, but the age band shown here (in **Chart 6.7**) is smaller, in that it only covers those between the ages of 15 and 19. This reflects a more general problem of being able to make comparisons across Europe given the wide variability of statistics collected in different countries and by different pan-European agencies.

It will be obvious that information on the rates of self-poisoning and self-mutilation – popularly referred to as self-harm – are more difficult to obtain than information on rates of completed suicide. However, a recent international study carried out by Nicola Madge and colleagues (Madge et al., 2008) has given a picture of how seven different countries compare on both actual self-harm and thoughts about self-harm. Figures in **Chart 6.8** illustrate differences between England and a variety of countries among 15-16 year-olds in their self-harm behaviour. These findings not only show that

young women have higher levels of self-harming thoughts and behaviours than young men, they also show that young people in England are at the higher end when compared with those from most other countries in this study.

One of the leading experts in the field, Professor Keith Hawton, has been studying those admitted to hospital as a result of self-harm in the Oxford region for a number of years now, and some of his latest findings (Hawton et al., 2008) show the pattern of self-harm among the 15-24 year age group over time. As can be seen from the information in **Chart 6.9**, rates for both young men and young women have varied somewhat, but have remained within the same parameters over a decade or so. Hawton and colleagues have also been able to show how self-harm is distributed among the age range from 15 to 24 and, in **Chart 6.10**, it can be seen that those aged 19 and 20 are more likely to be involved in self-harm than those in other age groups.

Turning now to the prevalence of psychiatric disorder, it is useful that over the past few years more evidence on this question has become available. First, Meltzer (2000) studied children up to the age of 15, and then this study was repeated by Green et al. (2005). We show first the most recent evidence on this question and, as can be seen in **Chart 6.11**, approximately 12% of boys and 10% of girls have some type of disorder. Conduct disorders and hyperkinetic disorders are higher in boys, while emotional disorders are higher in girls. This finding is in line with previous research in this field. In **Chart 6.12**, we compare figures from 1999 with those from 2004 and, as can be seen, there has been very little change over this five year period. This is an important conclusion, especially as there has been so much public debate about the possible deterioration over the past decades in the mental health of young people.

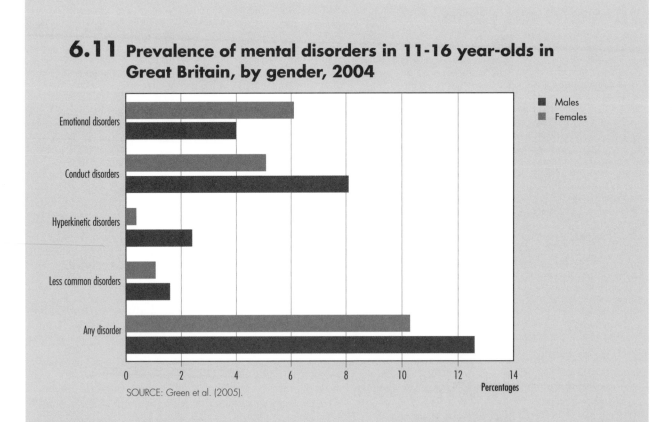

**6.11** **Prevalence of mental disorders in 11-16 year-olds in Great Britain, by gender, 2004**

SOURCE: Green et al. (2005).

**6.12** **Prevalence of mental disorders in 11-16 year-olds, in Great Britain, by gender, 1999 and 2004**

Percentages

|  | Boys | | Girls | |
|---|---|---|---|---|
|  | 1999 | 2004 | 1999 | 2004 |
| Emotional disorders | 5.1 | 3.9 | 6.1 | 6 |
| Conduct disorders | 8.6 | 8.8 | 3.8 | 5.1 |
| Hyperkinetic disorders | 2.3 | 2.6 | 0.5 | 0.3 |
| Any emotional, conduct or hyperkinetic disorder | 12.5 | 12.1 | 9.2 | 9.8 |
| Any disorder | 12.8 | 13.1 | 9.6 | 10.2 |

SOURCE: Green et al. (2005).

## 6.13 Prevalence of mental disorder among 11-16 year-olds, by ethnicity, 2004

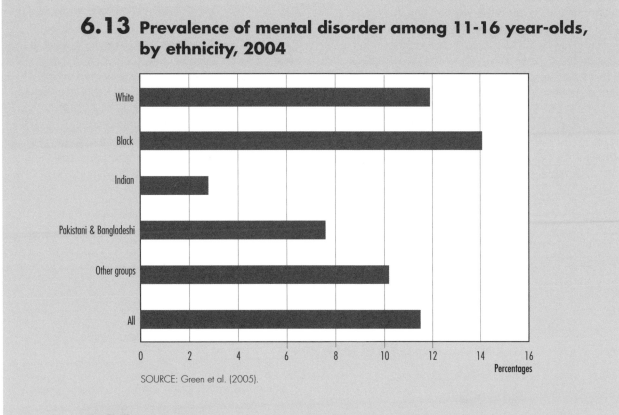

SOURCE: Green et al. (2005).

## 6.14 Prevalence of mental disorder among 11-16 year-olds, by educational qualifications of parent, 2004

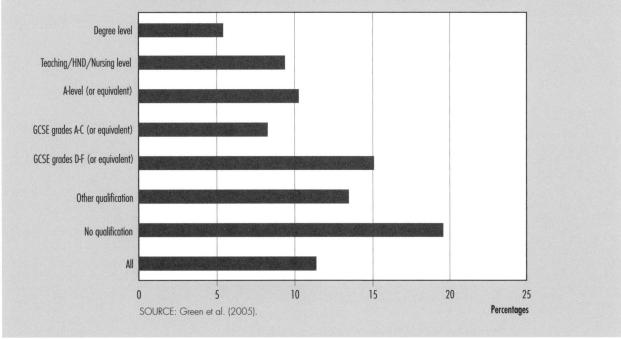

SOURCE: Green et al. (2005).

Returning to the 2004 cohort, this study provides a wealth of evidence on various aspects of psychiatric disorder, and two details of the findings are illustrated in **Charts 6.13** and **6.14**. In **Chart 6.13**, disorders are distributed according to ethnic group, and from this it can be seen that rates of disorder are higher among Black young people, and are very much lower among Indian adolescents. In **Chart 6.14**, disorders are distributed according to the educational qualifications

of the parent, a measure that is considered to reflect socio-economic status. These findings are particularly striking, illustrating how closely mental ill-health is associated with social background.

Another important area of concern in relation to mental health has been the situation of those in special circumstances and, in particular, those in custody and those in the care of the local authority. We will look at the situation of those in custody in Chapter 7, but for the moment we will look at those in care. It is only recently that reliable data on this subject have become available, indicating the scale of the problem and the vulnerability of those in this group. Figures in **Chart 6.15** show that 45% of those looked after by local authorities have some form of psychiatric disorder. As Ford et al. (2008) show, this compares with 14.6% of children and young people living in disadvantaged households, and with 8.5% of those in a community sample.

Whilst the study by Ford et al. (2008) does not distinguish by gender, previous studies of the in-care population have shown boys to have higher levels of disorder than girls. We note from **Chart 6.15** that the most common disorder is conduct disorder which, as we have seen in the general population (Chart 6.11), is more prevalent in boys than in girls. Figures in **Chart 6.16** show the differences between types of placement. Here it can be seen that rates of disorder are highest for those in residential care and lowest among those in kinship care and in foster care.

## 6.15 Percentage of children aged 5-17, looked after by local authorities, having different types of psychiatric disorder, in Britain, 2006

|  | Percentages |
|---|---|
| Psychiatric disorder | 45.3 |
| Emotional disorder | 12.4 |
| Conduct disorder | 37.7 |
| Hyperkinetic disorder | 8.4 |

SOURCE: Ford et al. (2007).

## 6.16 Proportions of children aged 5-17, looked after by local authorities, having psychiatric disorders by placement, in Britain, 2006

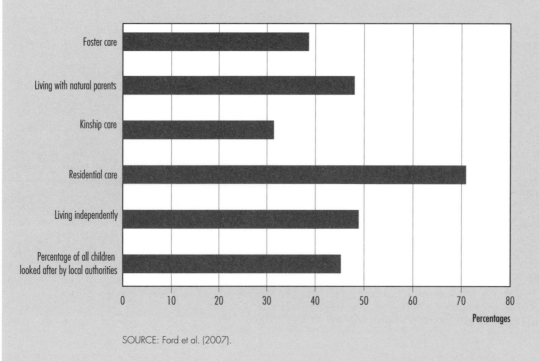

SOURCE: Ford et al. (2007).

Turning now to the problem of abuse, estimates vary widely as to the extent of this, and it is difficult to obtain figures which can be considered reliable. What is available is the number of those on child protection registers, and these are set out in **Chart 6.17.** From this it can be seen that there is an approximately equal distribution between the ages of 1-4, 5-9, and 10-15. Those who are over 16 form a small proportion of the total. It is also of note that there has been a reduction over a ten-year period in all age groups apart from those under the age of one. Changes in social work practice, as well as difficulties in the definition of abuse, have certainly contributed to this trend.

To conclude this chapter we will look at two sets of data concerned with general well-being. In the first set of data, derived from the HBSC study (Morgan et al., 2008), we consider the numbers of those who report feeling low weekly, across genders and across the four countries of the UK and Ireland. As can be seen in **Chart 6.18**, there is little change with age among boys, the figures in Scotland, Ireland and Wales remaining fairly stable between 13% and 18%. However, boys in England do appear to have increased levels of low mood, since their figures range from 21% to 26%. There is no obvious explanation for this, although it is perhaps worth drawing attention at

## 6.17 Number on Child Protection Registers, by age, in England, 1997-2007

Numbers

| | All ages | Under 1 | 1 - 4 | 5 - 9 | 10 - 15 | 16 & over |
|------|----------|---------|-------|-------|---------|-----------|
| | | | **Age at 31 March** | | | |
| 1997 | 32,400 | 2,800 | 9,800 | 10,000 | 8,700 | 810 |
| 1998 | 31,600 | 2,800 | 9,600 | 9,800 | 8,500 | 710 |
| 1999 | 31,900 | 3,000 | 9,700 | 9,700 | 8,600 | 650 |
| 2000 | 30,300 | 2,800 | 9,200 | 9,100 | 8,400 | 620 |
| 2001 | 28,600 | 2,800 | 8,000 | 8,000 | 7,400 | 560 |
| 2002 | 25,700 | 2,600 | 7,500 | 7,600 | 7,200 | 520 |
| 2003 | 26,600 | 2,800 | 7,600 | 7,700 | 7,600 | 510 |
| 2004 | 26,300 | 2,900 | 7,300 | 7,600 | 7,600 | 490 |
| 2005 | 25,900 | 3,000 | 7,400 | 7,400 | 7,300 | 490 |
| 2006 | 26,400 | 3,000 | 7,600 | 7,600 | 7,300 | 490 |
| 2007 | 27,900 | 3,200 | 8,200 | 7,700 | 7,800 | 610 |

SOURCE: Referrals, Assessment and Children and Young People on Child Protection Registers, England - year ending 31 March 2007.

## 6.18 Proportions of 11-15 year-olds who report feeling low weekly, by gender, in Great Britain and Ireland, 2006

Percentages

| | Males | | | | Females | | | | Both genders | | | |
|----------|------|------|------|------|------|------|------|------|------|------|------|------|
| | 11 | 13 | 15 | All | 11 | 13 | 15 | All | 11 | 13 | 15 | All |
| **England** | 21.6 | 24.0 | 26.8 | 24.0 | 27.0 | 36.2 | 45.7 | 35.9 | 24.4 | 30.3 | 36.5 | 30.2 |
| **Ireland** | 13.8 | 17.7 | 21.5 | 18.2 | 14.4 | 23.8 | 38.9 | 25.7 | 14.2 | 20.6 | 29.5 | 21.9 |
| **Scotland** | 12.7 | 13.0 | 15.3 | 13.8 | 16.6 | 23.2 | 32.6 | 24.6 | 14.8 | 18.2 | 23.9 | 19.3 |
| **Wales** | 18.3 | 16.5 | 19.6 | 18.1 | 22.4 | 27.3 | 35.5 | 28.1 | 20.4 | 22.0 | 27.6 | 23.2 |

SOURCE: Morgan, A et al. (in press 2008).

this point to the landmark UNICEF report (2007) which noted higher levels of poor emotional health among young people in Britain compared with their counterparts in other European countries.

Looking now at the girls in this sample, two things are apparent. Again, those in England score higher than those in other countries, but also among girls there is a clear developmental trend, with the numbers who report feeling low weekly clearly increasing with age. This is definitely an important finding, and raises questions about what can be done to improve the quality of life for many of our young people.

To provide additional depth to this picture of emotional health, we show in **Chart 6.19** some findings from the Balding (2007) study concerning young people's worries. From this it can be seen that, as we have just noted, girls worry more than boys, and that the extent of worries increases with age. Many adolescents worry about family and friends, but there is no doubt that exams and tests loom large for almost all age groups. Personal appearance (the way you look) is also a major issue for young women, and one that increases in salience with age, to the extent that 54% of 14-15 year-olds identify this as a matter of concern.

## 6.19 Proportions of 10-15 year-olds responding "A lot/Quite a lot" to the question: "How much do you worry about these problems?"

Percentages

|  | Males | | | Females | | |
|---|---|---|---|---|---|---|
|  | 10-11 | 12-13 | 14-15 | 10-11 | 12-13 | 14-15 |
| School-work problems | 15 | 22 | 28 | 14 | 25 | 39 |
| Exams and tests | 25 | 19 | 23 | 31 | 25 | 32 |
| Health problems | 20 | 28 | 24 | 20 | 34 | 31 |
| Career problems | * | 19 | 23 | * | 18 | 26 |
| Problems with friends | 16 | 23 | 22 | 24 | 40 | 38 |
| Family problems | 29 | 26 | 24 | 32 | 32 | 35 |
| Money problems | 8 | 18 | 20 | 7 | 17 | 23 |
| The way you look | 14 | 25 | 26 | 24 | 49 | 54 |
| Puberty and growing up | 11 | 12 | 9 | 20 | 17 | 13 |
| Bullying | 4 | 15 | 9 | 6 | 20 | 13 |
| Being gay, lesbian or bisexual | * | 5 | 4 | * | 4 | 3 |
| None of these | 43 | 37 | 33 | 36 | 22 | 16 |

* options not available

SOURCE: Balding (2007).

# References

Balding J et al. (2007)  *Young people into 2007.*   Schools Health Education Unit, University of Exeter.  Exeter.

Ford T et al. (2007) Psychiatric disorder among British children looked after by local authorities: comparison with children living in private households. *British Journal of Psychiatry.* 190.  319-325.

Green H et al. (2005)  *Mental health of children and young people in Great Britain, 2004.* Office for National Statistics. Stationery Office. London.

Hawton K et al. (2006) *Deliberate self-harm in Oxford, 2004.* Centre for Suicide Research, University of Oxford.

Hawton K et al. (2008) Adolescents who self-harm: a comparison of those who go to hospital and those who do not. *Child and Adolescent Mental Health.*  Blackwells Publishing.

Madge N et al. (2008) Deliberate self-harm within an international community sample of young people. *Journal of Child Psychology and Psychiatry.* 49.  667-677.

Meltzer H et al. (2000) *Mental health of children and adolescents in Great Britain.*  Office for National Statistics. Stationery Office, London.

Morgan A et al. (2008) *Health and behaviour in school-aged children (HBSC) Great Britain and Ireland report.* In Press.

.................... (2007)  UNICEF Report Card 7. *Child poverty in perspective: an overview of child well-being in rich countries.* February 2007.  Obtainable from www.unicef.org

# CHAPTER 7

## Crime

## Increased offending by young women

Although the number who are found guilty or cautioned for indictable offences has fallen among young men over the last decade, it is rising among young women between the ages of 12 and 17 (Chart 7.2)

## Numbers in custody

In 2008, there were 2,400 young people between the ages of 15 and 17 who were being held in custody (Chart 7.5)

## Ethnic differences

Significantly more young people from ethnic minority backgrounds receive custodial sentences than do young people from a White British background (Chart 7.7)

## Sharp fall in the use of ASBOs

The number of Anti-Social Behaviour Orders issued by the courts reached a peak in 2005 but fell back markedly in 2006 (Chart 7.13)

## Knife crime

In 2008, approximately 6% of 14-17 year-olds reported carrying knives over the past year (Chart 7.18)

# Crime

Youth crime continues to feature as a topic of major concern for both policy makers and for the general public. The apparent rise in knife crime and in the murders of young people in inner-city areas in the past two years has intensified the debate and raised major questions for Government about how to approach the subject of violent anti-social behaviour. Other topics of concern include the direction of the Youth Justice Board, the workings of the youth offending teams and the size of the prison population for juveniles and young offenders.

As part of this chapter we will look at some of the evidence collected in relation to these questions but we will begin by considering some background data on youth offending. Looking first at the peak age of offending, it will be clear from **Chart 7.1** that there is a significant difference between males and females in rates of offending. For young men, offending reaches a peak at age 17 while for young women, the peak occurs earlier at around 15 years of age.

As far as the numbers of young people found guilty or cautioned for indictable offences in the period 1996 to 2006 are concerned, it can be seen from the figures in **Chart 7.2** that there has been a decline for males, at least in the older two age groups. The opposite is true for females in the younger two age groups, particularly in the three years between 2003 and 2006. It could be argued that, since offending is much more common among males, the fall in rates among young men over a ten-year period is the finding on which we should concentrate. This is certainly true, and it is undoubtedly good news. To take a concrete example, for men in the 18-20 age group, the rate per 100,000 population has declined from 7,662 in 1996 to 5,626 in 2006.

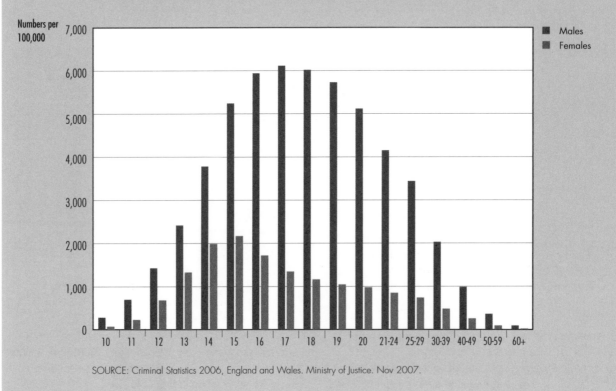

**7.1 Persons found guilty of, or cautioned for, indictable offences per 100,000 population, by age and gender, in England and Wales, 2006**

SOURCE: Criminal Statistics 2006, England and Wales. Ministry of Justice. Nov 2007.

**7.2** **Persons found guilty of, or cautioned for, indictable offences per 100,000 population, by gender and age group, in England and Wales, 1996-2006**

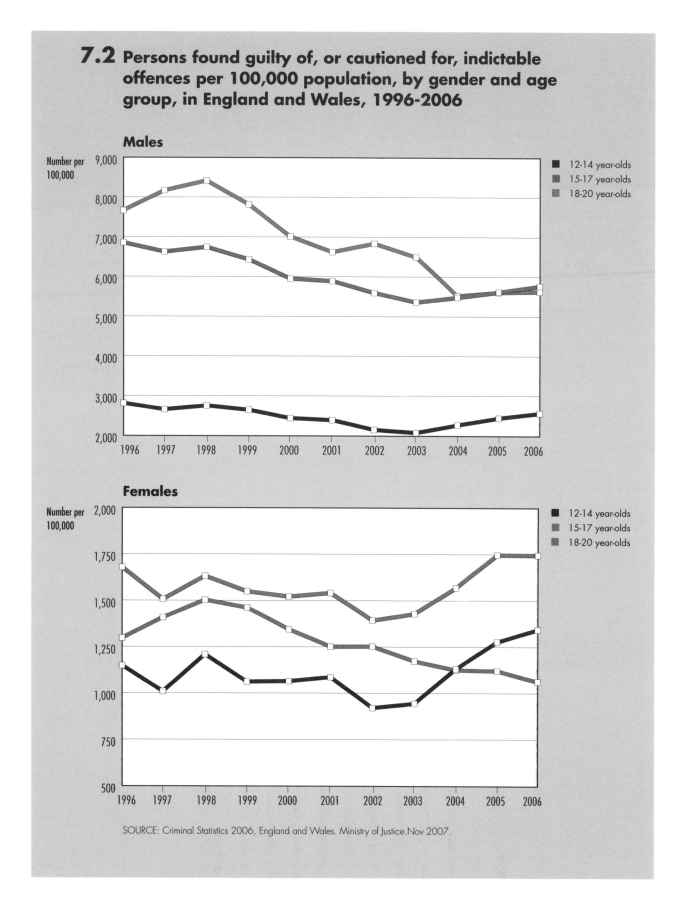

SOURCE: Criminal Statistics 2006, England and Wales. Ministry of Justice. Nov 2007.

Nonetheless, the rise in rates among young women, while relating to a much smaller number, is still of significant concern. The rates are only marginally higher than in 1996, but this is in spite of major efforts by those in the youth justice system and the introduction of a very wide range of measures aimed at prevention and early intervention. There is no doubt that crime among young women must be a serious issue for all working in this field.

Turning now to the proportion of those cautioned as a percentage of all who are found guilty, it will be seen from figures in **Chart 7.3** that there has been relatively little change in the use of this disposal by the courts over the last few years. This seems most likely to be the result of the introduction of a range of new community sentences, and the increasing variety of sentencing options available to magistrates in the youth courts.

A consideration of the data in **Chart 7.4** indicates how high a percentage of all offences among this age group involve theft and burglary. In the youngest groups, these offences account for over 50% of all offences, but this does reduce with age. It is also notable that drug offences as a proportion of all offences increase with age, especially in young men. Drug offences in men aged between 18 and 20 account for 15% of all offences in this age group, which is much the same as for violence against the person. The highest proportion of offences falls into the theft and handling stolen goods category.

## 7.3 Offenders cautioned for indictable offences as a percentage of offenders found guilty or cautioned, by year and age group, in England and Wales, 1996-2006

Percentages

| Year | Males | | | | | Females | | | | |
|------|-------|-------|-------|-------|-----------|---------|-------|-------|-------|-----------|
|      | 10-11 | 12-14 | 15-17 | 18-20 | 21 and over | 10-11 | 12-14 | 15-17 | 18-20 | 21 and over |
| 1996 | 94 | 77 | 51 | 35 | 26 | 99 | 91 | 72 | 50 | 44 |
| 1997 | 93 | 74 | 49 | 35 | 26 | 98 | 89 | 68 | 48 | 42 |
| 1998 | 91 | 72 | 48 | 34 | 24 | 97 | 88 | 67 | 46 | 39 |
| 1999 | 87 | 69 | 45 | 31 | 22 | 96 | 87 | 64 | 43 | 36 |
| 2000 | 86 | 68 | 43 | 29 | 20 | 95 | 86 | 63 | 41 | 34 |
| 2001 | 86 | 66 | 42 | 28 | 19 | 95 | 85 | 64 | 41 | 32 |
| 2002 | 83 | 63 | 41 | 29 | 19 | 94 | 84 | 62 | 41 | 35 |
| 2003 | 85 | 66 | 44 | 31 | 20 | 92 | 83 | 65 | 44 | 33 |
| 2004 | 85 | 67 | 45 | 30 | 21 | 93 | 86 | 68 | 48 | 36 |
| 2005 | 87 | 69 | 47 | 35 | 25 | 95 | 87 | 69 | 52 | 41 |
| 2006 | 89 | 70 | 49 | 38 | 29 | 96 | 88 | 71 | 56 | 44 |

SOURCE: Criminal Statistics 2006, England and Wales. Ministry of Justice. Nov 2007.

## 7.4 Offenders found guilty or cautioned by type of offence, gender and age group, in England and Wales, 2006

Thousands

| | Males | | | | Females | | | |
|---|-------|-------|-------|-----------|-------|-------|-------|-----------|
| | 12-14 | 15-17 | 18-20 | 21 and over | 12-14 | 15-17 | 18-20 | 21 and over |
| **Indictable offences** | | | | | | | | |
| Violence against the person | 5.5 | 12.2 | 12.9 | 49.8 | 2.3 | 3.3 | 2.1 | 10.1 |
| Sexual offences | 0.4 | 0.7 | 0.6 | 5.0 | 0.0 | 0.0 | 0.0 | 0.1 |
| Burglary | 3.2 | 6.7 | 4.5 | 13.9 | 0.3 | 0.6 | 0.3 | 0.8 |
| Robbery | 0.9 | 2.6 | 1.6 | 2.6 | 0.2 | 0.4 | 0.1 | 0.2 |
| Theft and handling stolen goods | 11.9 | 21.6 | 15.4 | 70.9 | 9.4 | 10.7 | 5.2 | 24.2 |
| Fraud and forgery | 0.2 | 1.0 | 2.0 | 14.3 | 0.1 | 0.5 | 0.8 | 7.3 |
| Criminal damage | 2.5 | 4.1 | 3.0 | 8.8 | 0.5 | 0.7 | 0.3 | 1.3 |
| Drug offences | 1.2 | 9.3 | 12.4 | 45.3 | 0.2 | 0.8 | 1.2 | 6.6 |
| Other (excluding motoring offences) | 0.9 | 4.1 | 8.5 | 36.9 | 0.2 | 0.8 | 1.1 | 5.9 |
| Motoring offences | 0.0 | 0.5 | 1.0 | 4.1 | 0.0 | 0.0 | 0.0 | 0.2 |
| **Total** | **26.7** | **62.7** | **61.9** | **251.5** | **13.2** | **17.8** | **11** | **56.8** |

SOURCE: Criminal Statistics 2006, England and Wales. Ministry of Justice. Nov 2007.

## 7.5 Proportion of 15-17 year-olds in prison on remand and under sentence, by gender, 2004 and 2008

Numbers

| September 2004 | Males | Females | Total |
|---|---|---|---|
| All 15-17 year olds in prison, of which | 2,229 | 65 | 2,294 |
| Remand | 488 | 12 | 500 |
| Under sentence | 1,740 | 52 | 1,794 |

| August 2008 | Males | Females | Total |
|---|---|---|---|
| All 15-17 year olds in prison, of which | 2,339 | 64 | 2,403 |
| Remand | 562 | 16 | 578 |
| Under sentence | 1,777 | 48 | 1,825 |

SOURCE: Population in Custody, Sept 2004, Research, Development and Statistics Directorate.
Population in Custody, August 2008, England and Wales. Ministry of Justice Statistics Bulletin.

## 7.6 Number of young offenders held in custody in England and Wales in 1995, 2002 and 2008, by gender

Numbers

| | 1995 | 2002 | 2008 |
|---|---|---|---|
| **Males** | 5,842 | 8,608 | 9,255 |
| **Females** | 183 | 464 | 399 |

SOURCE: Prison Statistics, Home Office, 2004; and Population in Custody, Development and Statistics Directorate, 2008.

In the last few years, there has been much public concern over the numbers of young people in custody in the UK. As can be seen in **Chart 7.5**, a comparison of 2004 and 2008 shows an overall increase from 2,294 to 2,403. This is not a major increase in numbers but, in a context where the stated aim of policy is to reduce the numbers of 15-17 year-olds receiving custodial sentences, this is not encouraging news.

As far as all young offenders up to the age of 21 are concerned, **Chart 7.6** illustrates the changes since 1995. Here it can be seen that since this time the numbers of males in custody has almost doubled, and for females it has more than doubled. Of course, this has to be seen in the context of the rise in the prison population generally but, nonetheless, it is undoubtedly one of the most shocking facts about life in Britain that we lock up so many of our young people in this way.

Another feature of offending policy that has raised concern in recent years is the distribution of offences according to the ethnic background of the offender. As will be apparent from **Chart 7.7**, White young people are significantly less likely to receive custodial sentences than those from other ethnic backgrounds. While it might be argued that the nature of the offence differs according to ethnicity, researchers do not believe that this is sufficient reason to explain the more frequent use of custody for Black and Asian young people.

Turning now to re-offending, **Chart 7.8** shows two-year rates for various age groups, including the 18-20 age group. It can be seen from this chart that the rate for this group is just below 70%, and has not changed that much among the three cohorts. Clearly this is a very high rate indeed and illustrates once again that, for most offenders, custody is very unlikely to offer rehabilitation and opportunities to desist from criminal behaviour.

## 7.7 Percentage of young people aged 10-17 years-old who received community and custodial sentences, by ethnic origin, during 2006/07

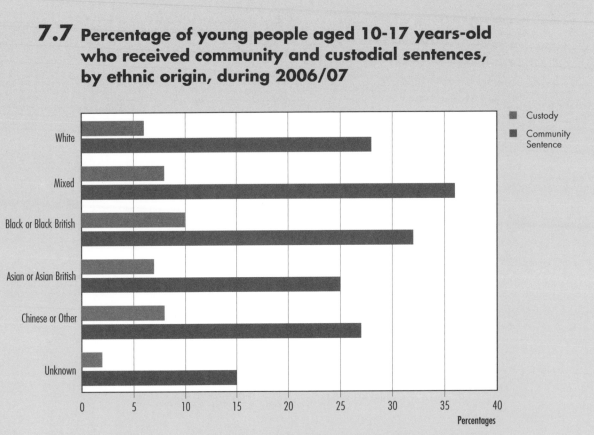

SOURCE: Statistics on Race and the Criminal Justice System. A Ministry of Justice Publication, July 2008.

## 7.8 Two-year re-offending rates by age of offenders, in England and Wales, 2000, 2002 and 2003

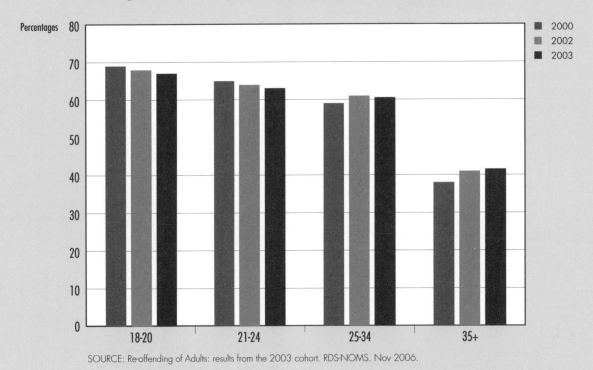

SOURCE: Re-offending of Adults: results from the 2003 cohort. RDS-NOMS. Nov 2006.

## 7.9 Two-year re-offending rates by offence group among 18-20 year-olds, by gender, 2004

Percentages

| | Females | Males |
|---|---|---|
| Violence | 44.4 | 56.7 |
| Robbery | 52.9 | 67.2 |
| Public order or riot | 36.7 | 53.9 |
| Sexual | * | 29.4 |
| Sexual (Child) | * | 48.6 |
| Soliciting or prostitution | * | * |
| Domestic burglary | 52.2 | 73.7 |
| Other burglary | 42.9 | 75.9 |
| Theft | 65.3 | 78.2 |
| Handling | 65.9 | 73.0 |
| Fraud and forgery | 46.2 | 47.9 |
| Absconding or bail offences | 69.0 | 78.0 |
| Taking and driving away & related offences | 85.7 | 71.5 |
| Theft from vehicles | * | 82.6 |
| Other motoring offences | 41.9 | 64.8 |
| Drink driving offences | 15.4 | 38.4 |
| Criminal or malicious damage | 50.0 | 65.8 |
| Drugs import/export/production/supply | 14.3 | 35.4 |
| Drugs possession/small scale supply | 29.6 | 52.4 |
| Other | 51.9 | 60.9 |

\* Data removed as extremely low numbers make the identification of individual offenders possible

Source: Re-offending of Adults: results from the 2003 cohort. RDS-NOMS. Nov 2006.

## 7.10 Psychiatric morbidity among male young offenders

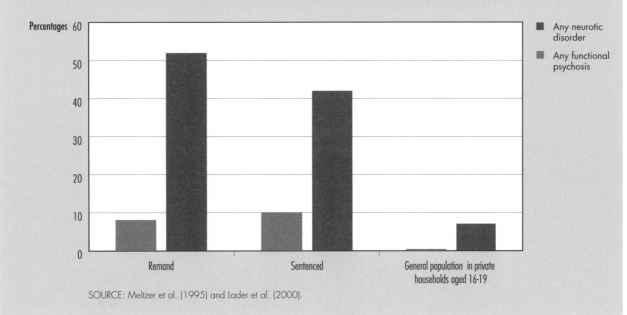

Percentages

■ Any neurotic disorder

■ Any functional psychosis

Remand    Sentenced    General population in private households aged 16-19

SOURCE: Meltzer et al. (1995) and Lader et al. (2000).

We can see in **Chart 7.9** that re-offending rates differ according to the offence itself. Thus, for example, vehicle-related crime has a particularly high rate of re-offending for both males and females, whilst fraud and forgery or violent crimes have lower rates of re-offending. This is an important consideration, and underlines the fact that not all criminal behaviour is the same. Prevention and early intervention programmes clearly need to take this into account.

The poor mental health of young offenders is a characteristic which has been highlighted in many of the reports on this population. One key study to have provided important information is that carried out by Lader et al. (2000). Some results from this research are illustrated in **Chart 7.10**. Figures are only shown for male young offenders, but from these it can be seen that rates of both functional psychosis and neurotic disorders are many times higher in this group than among the population as a whole (Meltzer et al., 1995). The sample of female offenders was too small in most categories to be able to draw any reliable conclusions but among sentenced young women, the rate of neurotic disorder was 68% compared with 19% in the general population.

Moving now from considerations of custody to more general issues to do with youth crime, it is well known that statistics in this field are open to all manner of criticism. One charge that is often levelled is that appearances in court are a serious underestimate of the true rate of offending. One way of getting round

this problem is to look at self-reported offending behaviour. Over the last ten years, there have been numerous such studies and in previous editions of this volume we have quoted from the Home Office, the Youth Justice Board and MORI, as well as from academic researchers. One recent study is the Home Office Offending, Crime and Justice Survey, published in 2006. Figures from this survey are shown in **Chart 7.11** and reflect clearly the link between being an offender and being a victim of crime.  At least as many young people are both offender and victim, as are offender only.

## 7.11 Proportion of offenders who were victims in the last 12 months, by age, 2006

Percentages

|  | 10 - 15 | | 16 - 25 | |
|---|---|---|---|---|
|  | **Offender** | **Non-offender** | **Offender** | **Non-offender** |
| Victim | 55 | 22 | 47 | 18 |
| Non-victim | 45 | 78 | 53 | 82 |
| Unweighted base | 485 | 1,284 | 647 | 2,400 |

SOURCE: Young people and crime: findings from the 2006 Offending Crime and Justice Survey. Home Office Statistical Bulletin, July 2008.

## 7.12 Proportion of young people committing anti-social behaviour, by age, in England and Wales, 2006

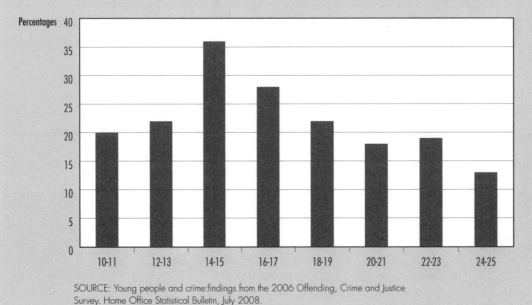

SOURCE: Young people and crime:findings from the 2006 Offending, Crime and Justice Survey. Home Office Statistical Bulletin, July 2008.

## 7.13 Number of anti-social behaviour orders (ASBOs) issued to persons aged 10-17 years-old, in England and Wales, 2001-2006

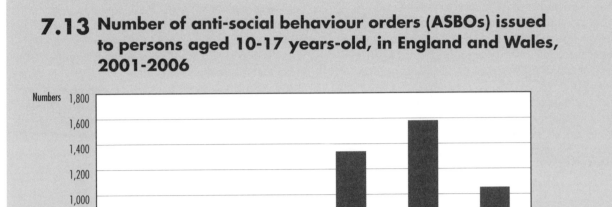

SOURCE: www.crimereduction.gov.uk. Anti-Social Behaviour Orders. Sept 2008.

## 7.14 Average time between arrest and sentence for persistent young offenders, in England and Wales, 1996-2007

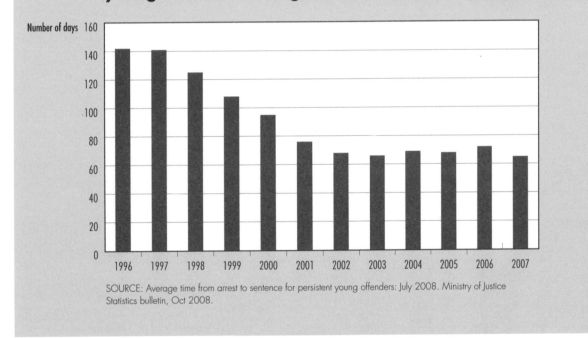

SOURCE: Average time from arrest to sentence for persistent young offenders: July 2008. Ministry of Justice Statistics bulletin, Oct 2008.

One distinctive feature of the Home Office survey is that it includes anti-social behaviour, a much wider category of behaviour than a criminal offence. Anti-social behaviour can include being rude or noisy in public, painting graffiti and other nuisance behaviour. As can be seen from **Chart 7.12**, approximately 36% of young people aged 14-15 say they have been involved in such behaviour. It is also of interest that the peak age for this is lower than the peak age of offending for young men, as was illustrated in **Chart 7.1**.

One of the most well-known disposals available to magistrates in recent years has been the notorious Anti-Social Behaviour Order, or ASBO. Figures in **Chart 7.13** indicate that this legal sanction has been used increasingly since it was first introduced in 2001, but its use has diminished somewhat since the high point of 2005. It will be of interest to see whether this downward trend has continued when further statistics become available.

One of the major commitments made by the Youth Justice Board since its inception in 1998 was a determination to reduce the time between arrest and sentence for persistent offenders. The criminal justice system had been severely criticised for this aspect of its work and the delay has been closely monitored ever since. Figures in **Chart 7.14** show that some considerable progress has been made in this area, with the average time between arrest and sentence coming down from 140 days in 1996 to roughly 60 days in 2007. Although there remains considerable

variation in the degree to which the courts meet their targets, nonetheless this is a considerable achievement and should be recognised as such.

We now turn to the question of victimization and to the evidence that young men in particular suffer as victims of crime. We have already noted the link between the two in **Chart 7.10** and it is important to record that males in late adolescence are not only the most likely group to be committing offences, but they are also the group most likely to be victims of violence. This can be

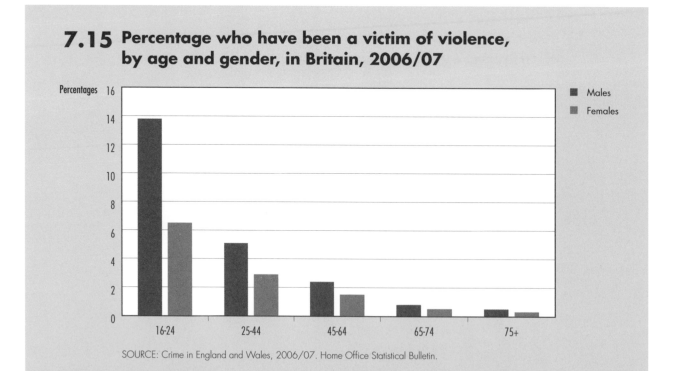

**7.15** **Percentage who have been a victim of violence, by age and gender, in Britain, 2006/07**

SOURCE: Crime in England and Wales, 2006/07. Home Office Statistical Bulletin.

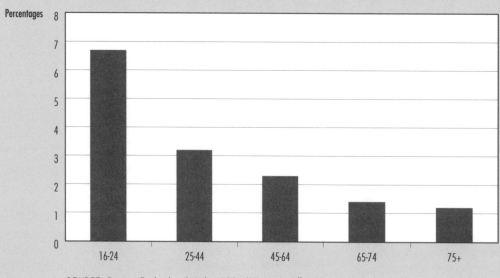

**7.16** **Percentage who have been a victim of burglary, by age, in Britain, 2006/07**

SOURCE: Crime in England and Wales, 2006/07. Home Office Statistical Bulletin.

seen from the data illustrated in **Chart 7.15** where it will be clear that the 16-24 year age group is significantly more vulnerable to violence than any other age group. It is also very striking that it is this group that is also more likely to be the victim of burglary, as can be seen from **Chart 7.16**.

In **Chart 7.17**, we show some very recent data collected by the London Authority concerning those who have been victims of rape and sexual offences in the London area. Here it can be seen that girls in the 0-17 year age group represent nearly one third of all

reported rape victims in the London area. In addition to this as an area of concern, there has also been much public anxiety over knife crime in inner-city areas, leading to debate about how to respond to such a trend. Figures in **Chart 7.18** illustrate the percentages of young people believed to be carrying knives and, as can be seen, the figures show around 6% of 14-15 year-olds and 16-17 year-olds to be doing so in the previous 12 months. These figures were collected as part of the Home Office Offending, Crime and Justice Survey, and were thus self-reported findings from young people themselves.

**7.17** **Among victims of rape and sexual offences, the proportions distributed by age group, in London, 2006/07**

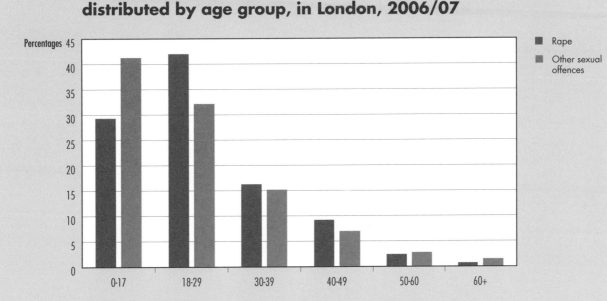

SOURCE: The State of London's Children Report, 2007. Greater London Authority, 2007.

**7.18** **Proportion of 10-25 year-olds carrying a knife in the last 12 months, 2006**

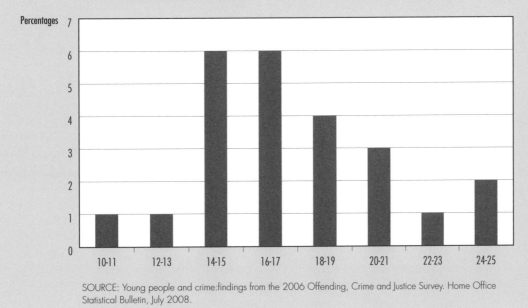

SOURCE: Young people and crime:findings from the 2006 Offending, Crime and Justice Survey. Home Office Statistical Bulletin, July 2008.

To conclude this chapter we consider the issue of the relationship between perpetrators and victims of assault. Figures in **Chart 7.19**, also collected as part of the Home Office Offending, Crime and Justice Survey, show that approximately half of all assaults,

whether they lead to injury or not, are carried out by perpetrators who are known to their victims. This is perhaps an unexpected finding and illustrates that a significant proportion of assaults are not random attacks but stem from already existing relationships.

## 7.19 Relationship between perpetrators of assault and their victims, among 10-25 year-olds, in a 12 month period, 2006

Percentages

| How well perpetrator known | Assault with injury | | Assault without injury | |
| | 10-15 | 16-25 | 10-15 | 16-25 |
| --- | --- | --- | --- | --- |
| Knew at least one well | 58 | 28 | 60 | 31 |
| Knew at least one by name | 22 | 15 | 19 | 13 |
| Knew at least one by sight | 8 | 10 | 9 | 8 |
| Not at all | 12 | 47 | 12 | 48 |

SOURCE: Young people and crime: findings from the 2006 Offending, Crime and Justice Survey. Home Office Statistical Bulletin, July 2008.

# References

Lader D et al. (2000) *Psychiatric morbidity among young offenders in England and Wales.* The Stationery Office. London.

Meltzer H et al. (1995) *The prevalence of psychiatric morbidity among adults living in private households.* OPCS Survey of Psychiatric Morbidity in Britain: Report 1. The Stationery Office. London.

Roe S and Ashe J (2008) *Young people and crime: findings from the 2006 Offending, Crime and Justice Survey.* Home Office Statistical Bulletin. Home Office. London.